THE
VIETNAM
WAR

THE VIETNAM WAR

INTERPRETING PRIMARY DOCUMENTS

Nick Treanor, Book Editor

Daniel Leone, President
Bonnie Szumski, Publisher
Scott Barbour, Managing Editor

GREENHAVEN
PRESS ®

THOMSON

GALE

San Diego • Detroit • New York • San Francisco • Cleveland
New Haven, Conn. • Waterville, Maine • London • Munich

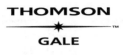

LIBRARY OF CONGRESS CATALOGING-IN-PUBLICATION DATA

The Vietnam War / Nick Treanor, book editor.
   p. cm. — (Interpreting primary documents)
  Includes bibliographical references and index.
  ISBN 0-7377-2263-0 (pbk. : alk. paper) — ISBN 0-7377-2262-2 (lib. : alk. paper)
   1. Vietnamese Conflict, 1961–1975—Sources. I. Treanor, Nick. II. Series.
DS557.4.V57 2004
959.704'3—dc21
                                               2003049058

CONTENTS

doing in Vietnam and face questions from the press
to which it might not have any answers.

Chapter 3: The Face of War

FOREWORD

In a debate on the nature of the historian's task, the Canadian intellectual Michael Ignatieff wrote, "I don't think history is a lesson in patriotism. It should be a lesson in truth. And the truth is both painful and many-sided." Part of Ignatieff's point was that those who seek to understand the past should guard against letting prejudice or patriotism interfere with the truth. This point, although simple, is subtle. Everyone would agree that patriotism is no excuse for outright fabrication, and that prejudice should never induce a historian to deliberately lie or deceive. Ignatieff's concern, however, was not so much with deliberate falsification as it was with the way prejudice and patriotism can lead to selective perception, which can skew the judgment of even those who are sincere in their efforts to understand the past. The truth, especially about the how and why of historical events, is seldom simple, and those who wish to genuinely understand the past must be sensitive to its complexities.

Each of the anthologies in the Greenhaven Press Interpreting Primary Documents series strives to portray the events and attitudes of the past in all their complexity. Rather than providing a simple narrative of the events, each volume presents a variety of views on the issues and events under discussion and encourages the student to confront and examine the complexity that attends the genuine study of history.

Furthermore, instead of aiming simply to transmit information from historian to student, the series is designed to develop and train students to become historians themselves, by focusing on the interpretation of primary documents. Such documents, including newspaper articles, speeches, personal reflections, letters, diaries, memoranda, and official reports, are the raw material from which the historian refines an authentic understanding of the past. The anthology examining desegregation, for instance, includes the voices of presidents, state governors, and ordinary citizens, and draws from the *Congressional Record,* newspapers and magazines, letters, and books published at the time. The selections differ in scope and opinion as well, allowing the student to examine the issue of desegregation from a variety of perspectives. By looking frankly at the arguments offered by those in favor of racial segregation and by those opposed, for example, students can better understand those arguments, the people who advanced them, and the time in which they lived.

The structure of each book in the Interpreting Primary Documents series helps readers sharpen the critical faculties the serious study of history requires. A concise introduction outlines the era or event at hand and provides the necessary historical background. The chapters themselves begin with a preface containing a straightforward account of the events discussed and an overview of how these events can be interpreted in different ways by examining the different documents in the chapter. The selections, in turn, are chosen for their accessibility and relevance, and each is preceded by a short introduction offering historical context and a summary of the author's point of view. A set of questions to guide interpretation accompanies each article and encourages readers to examine the authors' prejudices, probe their assumptions, and compare and contrast the various perspectives offered in the chapter. Finally, a detailed timeline traces the development of key events, a comprehensive bibliography of selected secondary material guides further research, and a thorough index lets the reader quickly access relevant information.

As Ignatieff remarked, in the same debate in which he urged the historian to favor truth over blind patriotism, "History for me is the study of arguments." The Interpreting Primary Documents series is for readers eager to understand the arguments, and attitudes, that animated historical change.

INTRODUCTION

Vietnam and the Cold War

Vietnam is a relatively small country, a thin strip of land running alongside the South China Sea on the eastern edge of the Asian mainland. Although it is not much larger than New Mexico, in its jungles was waged one of the most significant wars of the latter half of the twentieth century. The Vietnam War is unique, however, not because of the number of countries involved nor because of the number of people killed. Rather, the Vietnam War stands out in history because it was one of the few hot spots in what is known as the Cold War, a long struggle between the democratic and Communist countries that developed after World War II. From the American perspective, the overwhelming goal of the Cold War was to defeat communism, or at least stop it from spreading, and it is for this reason that Americans fought and died in Vietnam.

The Roots of the Cold War

The Cold War, of which the fight for Vietnam was such an important part, began just as World War II was ending. In that war, the United States and the Soviet Union were important allies in the fight against the Axis powers of Germany, Japan, and Italy. By 1945 the Soviet army had stormed and occupied Berlin, the German capital, where it was soon joined by American, British, and French troops. At a conference in Potsdam, however, which was convened to discuss what to do with postwar Germany, the deep differences between the Allies came to the surface. The Allies in war were on their way to becoming enemies in peace.

World War II killed over three hundred thousand Americans, but the nation as a whole emerged from the war stronger. It had an expanded industrial base, a booming economy, and sole possession of the atom bomb, the most destructive weapon ever invented. In contrast, the Soviet Union in 1945 was in ruins. The war had killed 27 million Soviets, destroyed seventy thousand villages and hundreds of cities, and wiped out much of the country's industry and infrastructure. Joseph Stalin, the Soviet leader, knew the United States was hostile to communism, and he was eager to protect the Soviet Union and maximize its influence in Europe, particularly Eastern Europe. The United States, for its part, was opposed to the Communist dictatorship and mindful of the USSR's enormous military power. Moreover, it was worried that Stalin intended to dominate all of Europe and perhaps the world.

Less than a year after World War II ended, three events occurred that heightened the mutual suspicion between the United States and the Soviet Union and helped entrench the hostility between the Communists and non-Communists that led to the Vietnam War. First, Stalin made murky references in a speech to his view that capitalism and imperialism made future wars inevitable. To some, he was merely repeating the Communist conviction that capitalism led to war. To others, however, especially in the United States, the speech was a veiled threat, a declaration of the USSR's military intentions. Next, at the request of his superiors in Washington, the American ambassador in Moscow, George Brennan, prepared a lengthy memo assessing the political mood in the Soviet Union. His eight-thousand-word telegram to Washington warned that the Soviet Union intended to expand across the globe and recommended a policy of containment. Finally, just a few days later, Winston Churchill gave a historic and ominous address in Fulton, Missouri. Churchill, who had been the British prime minister during the war, was widely respected in the United States. In his speech he attacked the Soviet Union and described the border between the Communist and non-Communist states in Europe as an "iron curtain." The vivid metaphor captured the American imagination:

> From Stettin in the Baltic to Trieste in the Adriatic, an iron curtain has descended across the Continent. Behind that line lie all the capitals of the ancient states of Central and Eastern Europe. Warsaw, Berlin, Prague, Vienna, Budapest, Belgrade, Bucharest and Sofia, all these famous cities and the populations around them lie in what I must call the Soviet sphere, and all are subject in one form or another, not only to Soviet influence but to a very high and, in many cases, increasing measure of control from Moscow. . . . Whatever conclusions may be drawn from these facts, and facts they are, this is certainly not the liberated Europe we fought to build up. Nor is it one which contains the essentials of permanent peace. . . . Except in the British Commonwealth and in the United States where Communism is in its infancy, the Communist parties or fifth columns constitute a growing challenge and peril to Christian civilization.[1]

Just as the United States had interpreted Stalin's speech as a threat, Stalin was upset by Churchill's speech, which he saw as a threat against the Soviet Union.

The shift from mutual suspicion to open, if contained, hostility did not occur until 1947. Postwar devastation and harsh winters had made life miserable for the people of Europe, and sympathy for communism spread, especially in France, Italy, and Germany. Britain had announced that it was unable to continue its military and economic support in Greece and Turkey, which bordered Communist regions. The United States felt it had to move quickly. In an address to Congress, President Harry Truman announced that henceforth the United States would oppose the spread of communism anywhere on the globe. The Truman Doctrine, as it became known, pledged American support for "free

peoples who are resisting attempted subjugation by armed minorities or by outside pressures."[2] The Cold War had officially begun.

Tensions between the Communist Soviet Union and the democratic West were highest in Germany, which had been divided after World War II into four zones, each of which was controlled by one of the major Allied powers. The United States, Britain, and France wanted a new, independent, and democratic German state, whereas the Soviet Union wanted Germany to remain weak, under control of the Four Powers, as the World War II victors were known. Eventually the country was divided into West Germany, allied with the United States and most of Western Europe, and East Germany, allied with the Soviet Union and most of the countries in Eastern Europe. In April 1949 the strategic alliance between Western Europe and North America became official with the creation of the North Atlantic

Treaty Organization (NATO). Under the terms of NATO, an attack on any member nation would be considered an attack on all member nations. The agreement deepened the divide between the Soviet Union and Western Europe. The divide became a gulf on August 29, 1949, the day the Soviet Union detonated its first atomic bomb. The world now had two nuclear superpowers, each of which was increasingly terrified of the other.

The Cold War Spreads to Asia

The year 1949 marked more than the Soviet entry into the nuclear age. It also marked the beginning of the Cold War in Asia, the place where, fifteen years later, hundreds of thousands of American soldiers would be sent in an effort to keep South Vietnam from falling to communism. In 1949 a Communist revolution led by Mao Tse-tung succeeded in overthrowing the government of Chiang Kai-shek, turning the world's most populous country firmly Communist. Although the focus of the Cold War remained Europe, where Communists and anti-Communists faced each other across a common border, the spread of communism into Asia was taken very seriously in the United States. The Soviet Union and China were both huge, powerful countries, rich in people and resources, and in size and influence they dominated Eurasia, the huge landmass that stretches from Ireland to Japan.

Also in 1949, Kim Il Sung, the leader of North Korea, first asked Stalin, the Soviet leader, for permission to invade South Korea. The Korea Peninsula had been divided after World War II into the north, controlled by the Soviet Union, and the south, controlled by the United States. In the years since the war the Soviets had installed Kim Il Sung, a Communist, in the north, and the United States had installed Syngmann Rhee, an ardent anti-Communist, in the south. Although Stalin initially declined Kim Il Sung's request for permission to invade the south, by 1950 he granted it, confident that Soviet possession of nuclear weapons and a friendship treaty between the Soviet Union and China would deter the United States from responding with military force to the spread of communism in Asia.

The Korean War

The United States responded, but not alone. It went to the United Nations Security Council to put together a UN force, made up of troops from sixteen countries, to defend South Korea. The Korean War was the first, but not the last, time America's commitment to prevent the spread of communism would lead it into war in Asia. In words that foreshadowed the conflict that would engulf Vietnam fifteen years later, President Truman explained to Congress in July 1950 why Korea was important: "Korea is a small country, thousands of miles away. But what is happening there is important to every American. The fact that communist forces have invaded Korea is a warning that there may be similar acts of aggression in other parts of the world."[3] The symbolic significance of Korea, like that of Vietnam years later, lay in the geopolitics of the Cold War. In itself it may have been a rather small battlefield, but it was a battlefield in a much larger and more important war.

The Korean War foreshadowed the Vietnam War in many other ways as well. Most importantly, perhaps, was the fact that the nature of Cold War alliances meant that in both places the United States waged a limited rather than a total war. Although the United States was much larger and more powerful than North Korea, just as it was much larger and more powerful than North Vietnam, in neither war could the United States use the full force of its military in an effort to win. Both times, doing so would have risked full-scale war with China and the Soviet Union.

Although the United States had expected an easy victory on the Korea Peninsula, its first attack was quickly repelled. However, after regrouping, and with the support of other nations, the United States recaptured the South Korean capital of Seoul. The South Korean army and the UN troops pushed northward, pursuing the fleeing North Korean troops. As they advanced into North Korea, however,

China became alarmed. North Korea was urging China to give it assistance, and the Soviet Union also pressed China to come to the defense of North Korea. On October 19, 1950, the North Korean capital of P'yongyang fell, and China soon ordered half a million troops to cross into North Korea toward the advancing American and UN troops.

A Limited War

The entry of China into the war caused deep concern in the United States. Just as it did in Vietnam years later, the United States chose to prosecute a limited rather than total war. Because of Cold War alliances, a full-scale attack on China may very well have led to World War III, drawing in the Soviet Union and its nuclear weapons. This was a risk the United States was not prepared to take. Consequently, President Truman refrained from using the atomic bomb and decided against launching attacks against China itself. In fact, Truman's commitment to limit the size of the war led him to fire General Douglas MacArthur, a war hero and the man in charge of conducting the Korean War, for insubordination. MacArthur had recommended that the United States bomb Chinese cities and was aggressively pressing to expand the war against China. Truman opposed these measures: "I believe that we must try to limit the war to Korea for these vital reasons. To make sure that the precious lives of our fighting men are not wasted; to see that the security of our country and the free world is not needlessly jeopardized, and to prevent a Third World War."[4] Chinese troops soon recaptured P'yongyang, the North Korean capital. They pressed on to recapture Seoul, the capital of South Korea, by early 1951, although UN forces recaptured Seoul two months later.

The struggle between the Soviet Union and the United States had changed the nature of war. Each country feared the other, and it was a fear that both motivated their hostility toward each other and kept it in check. Each side knew that a total war between the two superpowers would be unlike any other in history, involving nuclear weapons and unprecedented destruction.

The conflict in Korea foreshadowed the war in Vietnam not merely in how the United States fought it but also in how it ended it. By the summer of 1951 the two sides were at a standstill, and it became obvious that the United States was not fighting to win but rather was fighting for a negotiated peace. The war dragged on and casualties mounted, especially among North Korean civilians. In the 1952 elections Dwight Eisenhower replaced Truman as U.S. president, and the following year, with the death of Stalin, the Soviet Union got a new leader, too. A cease-fire deal was struck on July 27, 1953, and the first war between Communists and anti-Communists was over. The war had ended a stalemate. It had killed 54,000 Americans, 500,000 Chinese troops, and over 3 million Koreans (from north and south). China emerged from the war as a new power, yet the United States could claim a victory, too. It had contained the spread of communism and saved South Korea from communism. Even today, more than ten years after the end of the Cold War, the division between North and South Korea remains unchanged.

The Cold War Spreads to Vietnam

Just as the Korean War was ending, the focus in Asia shifted to Vietnam. In 1954 the French, who had ruled Vietnam since the late 1800s, finally were driven out of the country. Communist revolutionaries, led by General Vo Nguyen Giap, had won the country's independence after years of struggle. The Communists in Vietnam were nationalists, eager for an independent and strong Vietnam after so many years of colonial rule. They deeply resented the French and blamed them for controlling Vietnam and exploiting the country's people and riches. The United States, for its part, had been funding much of the French fight against the Vietnamese nationalists because it was ideologically opposed to communism.

At negotiations in Geneva, Switzerland, in 1954, the

various parties involved agreed to temporarily divide the country at the 17th parallel, with the Communists controlling the north and a pro-American ruler in charge of the south. The deal struck in Geneva called for a general election to reunite the country to be held within two years, but when the time came, Ngo Dinh Diem, who by then ruled South Vietnam and feared a Communist victory, refused to participate. Vietnam, rather than Korea, was emerging as the principal focus of Communist and anti-Communist conflict in Asia.

Although the main focus of American public interest and foreign policy remained in Europe, American involvement in Vietnam slowly grew. In a series of speeches during the 1950s, President Dwight Eisenhower, a World War II war hero, made it clear that the fate of Vietnam was an important part of the Cold War. Eisenhower held a view that came to be known as the Domino Theory, which predicted that if Vietnam fell to communism it would lead to Communist domination of all of Southeast Asia, as each country fell like dominos arranged in a row:

> We must recognize that whenever any country falls under the domination of Communism, the strength of the Free World—and of America—is by that amount weakened and Communism strengthened. If this process, through our neglect or indifference, should proceed unchecked, our continent would be gradually encircled. Our safety depends upon recognition of the fact that the Communist design for such encirclement must be stopped before it gains momentum—before it is again too late to save the peace.[5]

Historians today debate whether the Domino Theory was a sound one, with many claiming that it wrongly neglected important differences between Asian countries and overlooked the fact that smaller, less powerful countries had successfully remained independent of China for hundreds of years. Yet there can be no doubt that throughout the 1950s and 1960s, it was of enormous influence in shaping and justifying American policy in the Middle and Far East. In one way or another it remained influential for twenty years, as Presidents Eisenhower, John F. Kennedy, Lyndon B. Johnson, and Richard Nixon each endorsed the theory to explain and defend American activity in Asia. Starting with Eisenhower, who first articulated the Domino Theory, economic and military aid to the government of South Vietnam grew. From the American perspective, the United States was hewing to the commitment made years earlier by President Truman to contain communism wherever it was to be found. Vietnamese Communists, in contrast, saw American support for the South Vietnamese government as an effort to prop up an unpopular regime against the will of the Vietnamese people.

Cold War Crisis

Although the United States had an active interest in Vietnam throughout the 1950s, American involvement stepped up in the early 1960s, just as Cold War tensions reached their highest point. A couple of years earlier, relations between the Soviets and the West had actually eased. Nikita Khrushchev, who had replaced Stalin as head of the Soviet Union, even visited the United States in September 1959, becoming the first Soviet leader to do so. But the new spirit of cooperation ended when the Soviets discovered and shot down an American spy plane over Soviet territory. Khrushchev was outraged: "We don't want to threaten you, God forbid. But don't fly over the Soviet Union or the socialist countries. Respect our sovereignty and our borders. If you don't know where our borders are, we'll show you!"[6] Khrushchev demanded an apology from the United States, which the Americans refused to offer, and the tensions continued to mount. In 1961 the Soviets built the Berlin Wall between East Berlin, which it controlled, and West Berlin, which was controlled by the United States. The act outraged the United States, but there was little U.S. leaders could do.

The following year the situation grew even worse when the United States discovered the Soviet Union was shipping nuclear missiles to Cuba. The Kennedy administration was stunned to learn of the missiles via spy plane photographs. The missiles would have given the Soviets the ability to strike almost every American city with nuclear warheads without warning. As the administration debated its options, the fear of nuclear war was great. Finally, the Americans decided to impose a naval quarantine on the island. As American warships surrounded Cuba, the Soviet supply ships steamed toward the island and Americans began to prepare for nuclear war, stocking up wildly on supplies and preparing makeshift bomb shelters in their basements. Finally, Kennedy received a telegram from Khrushchev, in which the Soviet leader said that if the United States announced that it would not invade Cuba, "the necessity of the presence of our military specialists in Cuba will disappear."[7] A deal was struck, and the Soviet Union brought its missiles back home. The crisis eased, but the antagonism between the two superpowers that would lead to the Vietnam War remained.

Americans in Vietnam

The renewed intensity of the Cold War coincided with an increase in American support for the fiercely anti-Communist government of South Vietnam, which was unpopular with both Communists and non-Communists in the country. For some time the government of Ngo Dinh Diem had been fighting the National Liberation Front, a coalition of antigovernment forces, including Communists, and had been cracking down ruthlessly on dissenters. In 1961 Communist revolutionaries were emboldened by a Soviet announcement that it would support all wars of national liberation, and President Diem's grip on power grew more and more tenuous. In April, just a few months after the Soviet move, President Kennedy sent four hundred American soldiers to South Vietnam. The American "special advisers," as they were known, were in Vietnam not as combat units but to train and advise South Vietnamese troops.

Under President Kennedy, the United States increased its military and financial aid, hoping that a show of force in

Asia would strengthen its overall position in the Cold War. Some of the support was promissory, as when, in August 1962, Kennedy signed the Foreign Assistance Act, which pledged American military support for countries that bordered Communist areas and were under direct attack. But other support was immediate: Kennedy sought a limited partnership with President Diem and boosted the number of American military advisers in Vietnam to sixteen thousand. Throughout 1963, the final year of the Kennedy presidency, popular discontent within Vietnam grew as Buddhists staged rallies protesting President Diem's religious intolerance. The Kennedy administration grew disenchanted with Diem, and doubts began to surface about whether he was the best person for the job. In the fall, with Washington's quiet consent, elements within the South Vietnamese military staged a coup, deposing and later executing Diem. Whatever Kennedy's ambitions may have been in Vietnam, they were never allowed to play out, as he was assassinated in November of that same year.

The commitment to protect South Vietnam from communism continued under Lyndon B. Johnson, who succeeded Kennedy as president. Although Kennedy had introduced American troops onto Vietnam soil, they served a largely advisory role. Under President Johnson, in contrast, American troops first began to actively fight Communist forces—on the ground and in the air. In March 1964, just a few months after Johnson became president, Secretary of Defense Robert McNamara signaled American intentions: "We'll stay for as long as it takes. We shall provide whatever help is required to win the battle against the communist insurgents."[8] Revolutionary activity continued in South Vietnam, however, as Communists and non-Communists joined together to oppose a string of South Vietnamese governments, none of which were democratic and all of which, to varying degrees, used oppressive laws to restrict political dissent. The Communist government in North Vietnam, led by Ho Chi Minh, was similarly determined to overthrow the South Vietnamese regime and reunite Vietnam, and it actively helped the South Vietnamese revolutionary forces. As the South Vietnamese government struggled to hold onto control, more and more American military advisers were shipped to Vietnam. The war in Vietnam was one of gradual escalation; unlike in previous wars, there was no declaration of war by Congress. Instead, President Johnson, like President Richard Nixon after him, relied on the Gulf of Tonkin Resolution, which Congress passed in August 1964. The resolution gave the president authority to use whatever means were necessary to safeguard American troops in Vietnam. By 1965 American ground troops and bombers were involved. The Vietnam War, destined to become the longest war in American history, was underway.

The Cold War Influence

As with the Korean War, the Vietnam War was shaped by Cold War politics. The main American motivation in waging the war was to stem the tide of communism, which the United States feared would engulf all of Asia. Speaking in 1965, President Johnson said of the Communist revolutionaries, "Their target is not merely South Vietnam—it is Asia. Their objective is not the fulfillment of Vietnamese nationalism, it is to erode and to discredit America's ability to help prevent Chinese domination over all of Asia."[9] But as in Korea, Cold War politics determined that the Vietnam War could only be a limited war. Although the United States launched massive bombing campaigns against North Vietnam, it refrained from invading the north, aware that doing so might have provoked Communist China to get involved, just as it had fifteen years earlier in Korea. Similarly, although the head of the U.S. forces in Vietnam, William Westmoreland, had asked for permission to use tactical nuclear weapons to break a Communist siege of the American base of Khe Sanh, President Johnson refused. Whatever other motivations Johnson may have had, one of them certainly was that both the Soviet Union and China were nuclear powers; he was not going to use nuclear weapons against their Communist allies in Vietnam. The

Soviet Union and China, for their part, actively supported North Vietnam because it shared their Communist ideals. It was a poor country with little industry, so they supplied it with many of the arms it used against the American and South Vietnamese troops. To the people of Vietnam the war was personal: It was a struggle over the future of their country and over the kind of political and economic system under which they were destined to live. To the rest of the world, however, the war was a battlefield of ideologies in which one superpower openly fought a guerrilla force quietly supported by another.

Finally, again as in Korea, Cold War politics had a huge influence on how the war ended. The Korean War had ended in a stalemate and a negotiated peace, and in Vietnam the United States again found itself in a war that it could not win and yet could not afford to lose. Although the initial reports were promising, by 1968 it became clear that victory, if it came, would not be easy. In particular, the Tet Offensive in January of that year surprised most Americans, who had little inkling of the strength of the Communist forces. The Communists launched coordinated attacks on major cities throughout South Vietnam and even managed to seize control, briefly, of the American embassy in Saigon. Robert Kennedy spoke for many when he said,

> It is said the Viet Cong will not be able to hold the cities, and that is probably true. But they have demonstrated that despite all of our reports of progress, of government strength, and of enemy weakness, that half a million American soldiers, with 700,000 Vietnamese allies, with total command of the air, total command of the sea, backed by the huge resources and the most modern weapons, that we are unable to secure even a single city from the attacks of an enemy whose total strength is about 250,000.[10]

The Tet Offensive cost the Communists huge numbers of lives, and most of their attacks were quickly repulsed. If it was a military failure, however, it turned out to be a political victory because it helped convince the United States that the war would not be won easily.

Even after it became clear that the United States had little chance of being able to save South Vietnam from communism, Cold War politics made it difficult for the country to get out of the war. Although South Vietnam was of strategic importance, what was more important was the overall struggle against communism. The American aim shifted from saving South Vietnam to saving its own honor and showing the world and its Communist enemies that it was serious about fighting communism and that it would keep its commitments. The conflict in Vietnam stretched on for eight years, as the United States searched for a way to get out of the war without admitting failure. President Johnson realized in 1968 that the war would end not on the battlefield but at the negotiating table, and went ahead with peace talks. They collapsed, however, and it would take four more years, another American president, and hundreds of antiwar demonstrations before the United States got out of the war.

Although American involvement in the Vietnam War ended in 1973, the war itself did not end until 1975, when Saigon fell to the Communists. Vietnam was once again one country. The United States had embarked, a decade earlier, on an expensive and deadly mission that had ended in failure, as it was unable to prevent the Communists from taking control of South Vietnam. Whether and how much the American resolve to fight in Vietnam may have deterred the spread of communism is impossible to assess. Ultimately, however, America prevailed in the Cold War in 1991 with the collapse of the Soviet Union.

Notes
1. Winston Churchill, address at Westminster College, Fulton, Missouri, March 5, 1946. www.winstonchurchill.org.
2. Harry S. Truman, address to a joint session of Congress, March 12, 1947. www.ourdocuments.gov.

3. Harry S. Truman, message to Congress concerning Korea, July 19, 1950. www.pbs.org.

4. Harry S. Truman, press conference, April 11, 1951. http://wire.ap.org.

5. Dwight D. Eisenhower, address to the nation on the need for mutual security in waging peace, May 21, 1957. www.eisenhower.utexas.edu.

6. Nikita Khrushchev, address at Paris Summit, May 16, 1960. www.cnn.com.

7. Nikita Khrushchev, telegram to President Kennedy, October 26, 1962. www.sas.upenn.edu.

8. Robert McNamara, address in South Vietnam, March 9, 1964. www.pbs.org.

9. Lyndon Johnson, "Address to Members of the Association of American Editorial Cartoonists: The Challenge of Human Need in Viet-Nam," May 13, 1965.

10. Robert Kennedy, statement on the Vietnam War, February 8, 1968. http://www.intst.net/humanities/igcsehist/term5/vietnam/script.htm.

1

THE STRUGGLE
FOR INDEPENDENCE

CHAPTER PREFACE

The Vietnam War was not the first conflict between Vietnam and a Western power. In fact, the war between Vietnam and the United States developed out of a long conflict between Vietnam and France, which had conquered the small Southeast Asian nation during the 1800s. Like most other powerful European countries, France had developed an extensive overseas empire in which colonial rulers governed native populations, imposing a legal system, building public infrastructure, collecting taxes, and regulating the economy. By the middle of the twentieth century, however, most of the European empires had long been crumbling, and the French Empire was no exception. The balance of power in the world was changing, and France, which had been weakened by two world wars, could no longer sustain its position as a great power. For their part, many Vietnamese resented colonial rule and longed for independence.

In September 1945—just as World War II was ending—a Vietnamese revolutionary named Ho Chi Minh seized the initiative. With the broad support of the Vietnamese people, Ho Chi Minh declared Vietnam independent of France. His speech proclaiming independence clearly echoed the 1776 American Declaration of Independence and expressed the hope that the United States and other Allied forces would support his independence movement. The provisional government did not last long, however, as British troops arriving in the country quickly returned power to the French.

Ho Chi Minh and other Vietnamese revolutionaries continued to press for independence, using force when possible against French installations and working to gather support from ordinary Vietnamese. Finally, in 1954, France was driven out of Vietnam by a decisive defeat at Dien Bien Phu, a remote military base in the northwest corner of the country. Under the direction of General Vo Nguyen Giap, Vietnamese forces laid siege to French troops inside the base, cutting off their supply routes and forcing a massive surrender. French leaders realized that they could no longer maintain their colonies in Southeast Asia and met with Ho Chi Minh and other native Vietnamese leaders in Geneva, Switzerland, to negotiate the end of French rule.

The Geneva Convention of 1954 involved much more than a conflict between France and Vietnam. By then, the country had been caught up in the Cold War, a struggle for power between the Soviet Union and China, which were Communist, and the democratic countries of the world, led by the United States. In 1950 China and Russia had officially recognized Ho Chi Minh, who was Communist, as the leader of the Democratic Republic of Vietnam, based in the north. The United States and Britain responded by officially recognizing Emperor Bao Dai's government, which presided in the south under the direction of the French. Furthermore, China was shipping Ho Chi Minh military supplies, whereas the United States was sending France money for military aid. When the French and the Vietnamese, along with other interested parties, met in Geneva to decide the nation's future, most recognized that what was really at stake was whether the Communists would prevail in Vietnam.

In the end, the deal reached in Geneva called for the temporary division of the country into North Vietnam, ruled by Ho Chi Minh's Vietminh, and South Vietnam, ruled by Bao Dai. It also called for general national elections to be held within two years. By the time 1956 arrived, however, South Vietnam was ruled by Ngo Dinh Diem, who refused to allow the general election because he feared a Communist victory. The deadline for the election passed and Vietnam remained a divided country, with the Communists ruling the north and the American-backed Diem struggling to hold on to control of the south. The documents in this chapter explore the Vietnamese struggle for independence and offer various perspectives on the prospects for Vietnam in the wake of the Geneva Convention.

Vietnam Deserves Its Independence

Ho Chi Minh

On September 2, 1945, hundreds of thousands of people assembled in Hanoi to hear Ho Chi Minh declare Vietnam's independence. This event followed two weeks of uprising in which people throughout Vietnam called for a new government with him as its leader. In his address, Ho Chi Minh deliberately echoes the American Declaration of Independence and asserts that all people, including the Vietnamese, have the right to be free from the oppression he insists his country was made to endure. In particular, he is highly critical of the French, who conquered Vietnam during the mid-1880s and ruled until 1945. Ho Chi Minh, who was born Nguyen Tat Thanh, was a Vietnamese patriot and leader of the Democratic Republic of Vietnam. He was the chief force behind the Vietnamese struggle against French colonial rule and, later, against the Americans.

As you read, consider the following questions:
1. Why does Ho Chi Minh believe Vietnam has a right to be independent?
2. What complaints does he have about French colonial rule?
3. How does Ho Chi Minh believe the Allied nations (the victors in World War II) will respond to the Vietnamese declaration of independence?

All men are created equal; they are endowed by their Creator with certain unalienable Rights; among these are Life, Liberty, and the pursuit of Happiness.

Ho Chi Minh, *Ho Chi Minh On Revolution: Selected Writings, 1920–66*, edited by Bernard B. Fall. New York: Frederick A. Praeger, 1967.

This immortal statement was made in the Declaration of Independence of the United States of America in 1776. In a broader sense, this means: All the peoples on the earth are equal from birth, all the peoples have a right to live, to be happy and free.

The Declaration of the French Revolution made in 1791 on the Rights of Man and the Citizen also states: "All men are born free and with equal rights, and must always remain free and have equal rights." Those are undeniable truths.

Nevertheless, for more than eighty years, the French imperialists, abusing the standard of Liberty, Equality, and Fraternity, have violated our Fatherland and oppressed our fellow citizens. They have acted contrary to the ideals of humanity and justice.

In the field of politics, they have deprived our people of every democratic liberty.

They have enforced inhuman laws; they have set up three distinct political regimes in the North, the Center, and the South of Viet-Nam in order to wreck our national unity and prevent our people from being united.

They have built more prisons than schools. They have mercilessly slain our patriots; they have drowned our uprisings in rivers of blood.

They have fettered public opinion; they have practiced obscurantism against our people.

To weaken our race they have forced us to use opium and alcohol.

In the field of economics, they have fleeced us to the backbone, impoverished our people and devastated our land.

They have robbed us of our rice fields, our mines, our forests, and our raw materials. They have monopolized the issuing of bank notes and the export trade.

They have invented numerous unjustifiable taxes and reduced our people, especially our peasantry, to a state of extreme poverty.

They have hampered the prospering of our national bourgeoisie; they have mercilessly exploited our workers.

In the autumn of 1940, when the Japanese fascists violated Indochina's territory to establish new bases in their fight against the Allies, the French imperialists went down on their bended knees and handed over our country to them.

A People Oppressed

Thus, from that date, our people were subjected to the double yoke of the French and the Japanese. Their sufferings and miseries increased. The result was that, from the end of last year to the beginning of this year, from Quang Tri Province to the North of Viet-Nam, more than two million of our fellow citizens died from starvation. On March 9 [1945], the French troops were disarmed by the Japanese. The French colonialists either fled or surrendered, showing that not only were they incapable of "protecting" us, but that, in the span of five years, they had twice sold our country to the Japanese.

On several occasions before March 9, the Viet Minh League [which favored Vietnamese independence] urged the French to ally themselves with it against the Japanese. Instead of agreeing to this proposal, the French colonialists so intensified their terrorist activities against the Viet Minh members that before fleeing they massacred a great number of our political prisoners detained at Yen Bay and Cao Bang.

Notwithstanding all this, our fellow citizens have always manifested toward the French a tolerant and humane attitude. Even after the Japanese *Putsch* [attempt to overthrow the government] of March, 1945, the Viet Minh League helped many Frenchmen to cross the frontier, rescued some of them from Japanese jails, and protected French lives and property.

From the autumn of 1940, our country had in fact ceased to be a French colony and had become a Japanese possession.

After the Japanese had surrendered to the Allies, our whole people rose to regain our national sovereignty and to found the Democratic Republic of Viet-Nam.

The truth is that we have wrested our independence from

the Japanese and not from the French.

The French have fled, the Japanese have capitulated, Emperor Bao Dai has abdicated. Our people have broken the chains which for nearly a century have fettered them and have won independence for the Fatherland. Our people at the same time have overthrown the monarchic regime that has reigned supreme for dozens of centuries. In its place has been established the present Democratic Republic.

For these reasons, we, members of the Provisional Government, representing the whole Vietnamese people, declare that from now on we break off all relations of a colonial character with France; we repeal all the international obligation that France has so far subscribed to on behalf of Viet-Nam, and we abolish all the special rights the French have unlawfully acquired in our Fatherland.

The whole Vietnamese people, animated by a common purpose, are determined to fight to the bitter end against any attempt by the French colonialists to reconquer their country.

We are convinced that the Allied nations, which at [conferences in] Teheran and San Francisco have acknowledged the principles of self-determination and equality of nations, will not refuse to acknowledge the independence of Viet-Nam.

A people who have courageously opposed French domination for more than eighty years, a people who have fought side by side with the Allies against the fascists during these last years, such a people must be free and independent.

For these reasons, we, members of the Provisional Government of the Democratic Republic of Viet-Nam, solemnly declare to the world that Viet-Nam has the right to be a free and independent country—and in fact it is so already. The entire Vietnamese people are determined to mobilize all their physical and mental strength, to sacrifice their lives and property in order to safeguard their independence and liberty.

The Communists Will Likely Prevail in Vietnam

New Republic

The Geneva Convention of 1954 brought an end to years of fighting between the Vietminh, the Communist revolutionaries seeking to expel the French colonial forces, and France, which had been struggling to hold onto its colonial empire with the financial help of the United States. The agreement signed by the Vietminh and the French called for the temporary division of Vietnam into two zones. The Vietminh under Ho Chi Minh were to control the area north of the seventeenth parallel, while Bao Dai, the Vietnamese emperor who had ruled under the French, was to continue ruling in the south. Included in the agreement were provisions for a general election in 1956, after which the winning party would rule all of Vietnam. In the following editorial, the American magazine *New Republic* comments on the agreement, which it sees as a major diplomatic failure for the non-Communist world.

As you read, consider the following questions:
1. According to the *New Republic*, what are the pros and cons of the agreement, from the perspective of the negotiators on the French side?
2. What reasons does the article give for thinking the division of Vietnam at the seventeenth parallel is a natural one?
3. What does the *New Republic* predict will happen during the general elections scheduled for 1956?

The New Republic, "Can South Asia Be Saved?" *The New Republic*, vol. 132, August 2, 1954, pp. 7–8.

The Geneva Conference was a great diplomatic defeat for the non-Communist world. And while a military defeat is retrievable, there is a finality to a diplomatic defeat that cannot be overcome. Far more was salvaged from the ruins of colonialism in Indo-China than the French had any right to demand or reason to expect. In return the signatories of the truce agreement grant what the United States refuses to recognize—the permanence and strength of Communist China. From this act a new era may follow.

In the emergence of this new era lies the real significance of Geneva. But first it is worth assessing the good and the bad in the truce agreement itself. In praise of the negotiators it should be said that four gains are registered that do not reflect French power:

The French are given 300 days to leave Haiphong;

The Viet-Minh forces agree to withdraw from Laos;

The Communist-led Khmer Resistance Forces are to be disbanded in Cambodia;

Viet-Nam itself is divided close to the Seventeenth Parallel.

Assessing the Truce Agreement

The first of these gains permits France to salvage material and men that would have fallen into Communist hands, and gives her time to reassert herself in Europe. In other hands time has been wasted in Paris. But France's new found leader by moving at once on EDC [European Defence Community] and by granting immediate independence to Viet-Nam, has shown that he will make use of the time.

The second gain is more doubtful. Northern Laos is the natural base of operations for Communist expansion toward Thailand, Burma and the rest of South Asia. There is no way in which the Laos government can drive the Communist forces from that territory, and would be utopian to suppose that they will withdraw.

The third gain is more promising. Cambodia alone emerges unscathed from the truce agreement and that in turn reflects the militancy of its leadership and the unity of the nation. Yet the state is too small to survive long unprotected. The plains and marshes that make up its borders are indefensible, and only if India and Burma speak for it can it live.

Lastly, the division of Viet-Nam is a real, if momentary, concession by the Communists. Eighty percent of the illiterate people of Viet-Nam would choose Ho Chi Minh, if pic-

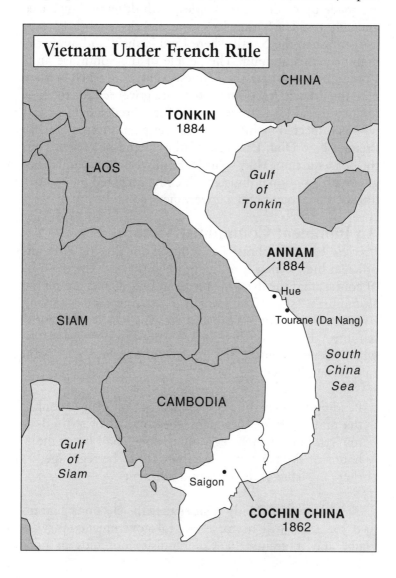

tures of Ho and Bao Dai were placed before them in a free election. Yet 50 percent of the people, by consent of the Communists, remain under Viet-Namese rule. Nor is the truncated state of Viet-Nam as absurd as it appears to be on first sight. Northern and Southern Viet-Nam were traditionally held separate under Chinese and French rule. They are made up of different peoples, with different languages and cultures. The South is a substantial rice exporting area, in contrast to the North where food is short and hunger is imminent this autumn. The people of the South are anti-Communist and hate the Chinese almost as much as they hate the French. In addition, they are governed for the first time by a real leader; one who is not a French citizen, and who is respected by his people for resistance to the French. Premier Ngo Dinh Dien is a Catholic, and he comes from the border area of Hue; so he lacks universal appeal. He begins with a national disaster which he accepted only under duress. But around him a government could be built.

An Imminent Communist Victory

It could be—that phrase has induced one illusion after another in Indo-China over the last eight years. The truth is, of course, that the dynamic forces in Indo-China are on the Communist side. The North is strong and growing stronger. The South is weak and growing weaker. And written into the terms of the military truce is a political clause which seems to ensure the transfer of Southern Viet-Nam to Communist rule:

> Pending the general elections which will bring about the unification of Viet-Nam, the conduct of civil administration in each regrouping zone shall be in the hands of the party whose forces are to be regrouped there in virtue of the present agreement.

This clause apparently ensures that the elections guaranteed for 1956 will be for a central government for Viet-Nam, and it grants the Communists footholds in non-

Communist territory until the elections are held. It seems inconceivable that anti-Communist candidates will venture to run for office in Communist-ruled areas. It is equally hard to believe that governments as weak as the Viet-Namese can survive while Communist candidates campaign for election in every village council or assembly district. The prestige of the Viet-Minh is enormous. The whole movement of history is toward the Viet-Minh side. The least that the Viet-Minh can hope for following the elections is a coalition government heavily dominated by Communists.

Barring a political miracle brought about by liberation from France, economic aid from America and the emergence of a local will to survive free, it seems certain that, by the terms of the truce agreement, the Communist conquest of Viet-Nam may be simply delayed for two years, and then brought about legally with the assent of the West.

The United States Will Stand by South Vietnam

Walter S. Robertson

At the 1954 Geneva Convention, the Vietminh general Ta Quang Buu and French general Henri Delteil signed the Agreement on the Cessation of Hostilities, which called for the temporary division of Vietnam at the seventeen parallel, followed by nationwide elections to be held in 1956. The deal was resisted by the United States and by the government of Bao Dai, the last emperor of Vietnam who ruled under French control, because it was widely thought that the Communist Vietminh would handily win in the 1956 national election. In 1955 Ngo Dinh Diem, who had defeated Bao Dai in a rigged election for control of South Vietnam, announced that he would refuse to participate in the planned election, and the deadline set by the Geneva Convention passed with no general election being held. In the following address to the American Friends of Viet-Nam, which occurred one month before the scheduled election date, Assistant Secretary of State for Far Eastern Affairs Walter S. Robertson lays out American policy in respect to Vietnam and pledges continued support for the Diem government.

As you read, consider the following questions:
1. What three stages in the recent history of Vietnam does Robertson identify?
2. What does Robertson announce as American policy in Vietnam?
3. In which area does Robertson say South Vietnam is weaker than North Vietnam?

Walter S. Robertson, address to the American Friends of Viet-Nam at the Willard Hotel, Washington, DC, June 1, 1956.

This past March [1956], I had the pleasure of accompanying the Secretary of State [John Foster Dulles] on his visit to Saigon where we conversed with President Diem on the present and future problems of Viet-Nam. I was struck, as so many other recent observers have been, at the progress Free Viet-Nam [South Vietnam] has made in a few short months toward stability, security, and strength. President Diem seemed to reflect this progress in his own person. On the occasion of our earlier visit some 15 months ago, he seemed tense and gravely concerned about the problems facing Viet-Nam. This time he was reposed, poised, and appeared confident of the future of his country.

Among the factors that explain the remarkable rise of Free Viet-Nam from the shambles created by 8 years of murderous civil and international war, the division of the country at Geneva and the continuing menace of predatory communism, there is in the first place the dedication, courage, and resourcefulness of President Diem himself. In him, his country has found a truly worthy leader whose integrity and devotion to his country's welfare have become generally recognized among his people. Asia has given us in President Diem another great figure, and the entire free world has become the richer for his example of determination and moral fortitude. There is no more dramatic example of this fortitude than President Diem's decisions during the tense and vital days of the battle against the parasitic politico-religious sects in the city of Saigon in the spring of 1955. These decisions were to resist the multiple pressures to compromise that were building up around him, and to struggle to the victorious end for the sake of a just cause. The free world owes him a debt of gratitude for his determined stand at that fateful hour.

Three Stages of History

Consider Viet-Nam at three stages in its recent history:

First, in mid-1954, partitioned by fiat of the great powers against the will of the Vietnamese people, devoid of governmental machinery or military strength, drifting without leadership and without hope in the backwash of the defeat administered by the combined weight of Communist-impressed infantry and of Chinese and Russian arms.

Secondly, in early 1955, faced with the military and subversive threat of the Communists north of the 17th parallel, confronted with internal strife, its government challenged by the armed, self-seeking politico-religious sects, its army barely reformed and of uncertain loyalty, assailed from within by the most difficult problems, including that of having to absorb the sudden influx of three-quarters of a million refugees who would rather leave their ancestral lands and homes than suffer life under Communist tyranny:

And finally Viet-Nam today, in mid-1956, progressing rapidly to the establishment of democratic institutions by elective processes, its people resuming peaceful pursuits, its army growing in effectiveness, sense of mission, and morale, the puppet Vietnamese politicians discredited, the refugees well on the way to permanent resettlement, the countryside generally orderly and calm, the predatory sects eliminated and their venal leaders exiled or destroyed.

Perhaps no more eloquent testimony to the new state of affairs in Viet-Nam could be cited than the voice of the people themselves as expressed in their free election of last March. At that time the last possible question as to the feeling of the people was erased by an overwhelming majority for President Diem's leadership. The fact that the Viet Minh was unable to carry out its open threats to sabotage these elections is impressive evidence of the stability and prestige of the government.

America: A Friend of Viet-Nam

The United States is proud to be on the side of the effort of the Vietnamese people under President Diem to establish freedom, peace, and the good life. The United States wishes to continue to assist and to be a loyal and trusted friend of Viet-Nam.

Our policies in Viet-Nam may be simply stated as follows:

To support a friendly non-Communist government in Viet-Nam and to help it diminish and eventually eradicate Communist subversion and influence.

To help the Government of Viet-Nam establish the forces necessary for internal security.

To encourage support for Free Viet-Nam by the non-Communist world.

To aid in the rehabilitation and reconstruction of a country and people ravaged by 8 ruinous years of civil and international war.

Our efforts are directed first of all toward helping to sustain the internal security forces consisting of a regular army of about 150,000 men, a mobile civil guard of some 45,000, and local defense units which are being formed to give protection against subversion on the village level. We are providing budgetary support and equipment for these forces and have a mission assisting the training of the army. We are also helping to organize, train, and equip the Vietnamese police force. The refugees who have fled to South Viet-Nam to escape the Viet Minh are being resettled on productive lands with the assistance of funds made available by our aid program. In various ways our aid program also provides assistance to the Vietnamese Government designed to strengthen the economy and provide a better future for the common people of the country. The Vietnamese are increasingly giving attention to the basic development of the Vietnamese economy and to projects that may contribute directly to that goal. We give our aid and counsel to this program only as freely invited.

I do not wish to minimize the magnitude of the task that still remains and of the problems that still confront this staunch and valiant member of the free world fighting for its independence on the threshold of the Communist heartland of Asia.

The Communist conspiracy continues to threaten Free Viet-Nam. With monstrous effrontery, the Communist conspirators at Hanoi accuse Free Viet-Nam and its friends of violating the armistice provisions which the Vietnamese, and their friends, including ourselves, have scrupulously respected despite the fact that neither the Vietnamese nor ourselves signed the Geneva Accords while they, the Communists who have solemnly undertaken to be bound by these provisions, have violated them in the most blatant fashion.

An Uncertain Future

The facts are that while on the one hand the military potential of Free Viet-Nam has been drastically reduced by the withdrawal of nearly 200,000 members of the French Expeditionary Corps and by the reduction of the Vietnamese Army by more than 50,000 from the time of the armistice to the present as well as by the outshipment from Viet-Nam since the cessation of hostilities of over $200 million worth of war equipment, we have on the other hand reports of steady constant growth of the warmaking potential of the Communists north of the 17th parallel.

Our reports reveal that in complete disregard of its obligations, the Viet Minh have imported voluminous quantities of arms across the Sino-Viet Minh border and have imported a constant stream of Chinese Communist military personnel to work on railroads, to rebuild roads, to establish airports, and to work on other projects contributing to the growth of the military potential of the zone under Communist occupation.

As so eloquently stated by the British Government in a diplomatic note released to the press and sent to Moscow in April of this year, and I quote:

> The Viet Minh army has been so greatly strengthened by the embodiment and re-equipment of irregular forces that instead of the 7 Viet Minh divisions in existence in July 1954 there are now no less than 20. This striking contrast between massive military expansion in the North and the withdrawal and reduction of military forces in the South speaks for itself.

> By lies, propaganda, force, and deceit, the Communists

in Hanoi would undermine Free Viet-Nam, whose fall they have been unable to secure by their maneuverings on the diplomatic front. These people, whose crimes against suffering humanity are so vividly described in the book by Lt. [Tom] Dooley [author of *Deliver Us from Evil*] who addressed you this morning, have sold their country to Peiping [Beijing]. They have shamelessly followed all the devious zigzags of the Communist-bloc line so that their alliance with Communist China and the Soviet Union is firmly consolidated. These are the people who are now inviting President Diem to join them in a coalition government to be set up through so-called "free elections."

President Diem and the Government of Free Viet-Nam reaffirmed on April 6 of this year and on other occasions their desire to seek the reunification of Viet-Nam by peaceful means. In this goal, we support them fully. We hope and pray that the partition of Viet-Nam, imposed against the will of the Vietnamese people, will speedily come to an end. For our part we believe in free elections, and we support President Diem fully in his position that if elections are to be held, there first must be conditions which preclude intimidation or coercion of the electorate. Unless such conditions exist there can be no free choice.

May those leaders of the north in whom the spirit of true patriotism still survives realize the futility of the Communist efforts to subvert Free Viet-Nam by force or guile. May they force the abandonment of these efforts and bring about the peaceful demobilization of the large standing armies of the Viet Minh. May they, above all, return to the just cause of all those who want to reunify their country in peace and independence and for the good of all the people of Viet-Nam.

A United Front Against Fascism in South Vietnam

National Liberation Front of South Vietnam

On December 20, 1960, the National Liberation Front, composed of both Communists and non-Communist dissident groups, was formed in South Vietnam to oppose the presidency of Ngo Dinh Diem. It enjoyed the support of the North Vietnamese government, and along with its militant wing, known as the Vietcong, fought against the South Vietnamese government and the United States. The following document lays out the program of the National Liberation Front.

As you read, consider the following questions:
1. How does the National Liberation Front characterize the relationship between the government of South Vietnam and the United States?
2. What major legal, economic, and social changes does the National Liberation Front advocate?
3. What is the attitude of the National Liberation Front toward war, according to the document?

I. Overthrow the camouflaged colonial regime of the American imperialists and the dictatorial power of Ngo Dinh Diem [president of South Vietnam], servant of the Americans, and institute a government of national democratic union.

The present South Vietnamese regime is a camouflaged colonial regime dominated by the Yankees, and the South Vietnamese government is a servile government, imple-

National Liberation Front of South Vietnam, "Program of the National Liberation Front of South Vietnam," http://vietnam.vassar.edu.

menting faithfully all the policies of the American imperialists. Therefore, this regime must be overthrown and a government of national and democratic union put in its place composed of representatives of all social classes, of all nationalities, of various political parties, of all religions; patriotic, eminent citizens must take over for the people the control of economic, political, social, and cultural interests and thus bring about independence, democracy, well-being, peace, neutrality, and efforts toward the peaceful unification of the country.

II. *Institute a largely liberal and democratic regime.*

1. Abolish the present constitution of the dictatorial powers of Ngo Dinh Diem, servant of the Americans. Elect a new National Assembly through universal suffrage.

2. Implement essential democratic liberties: freedom of opinion, of press, of movement, of trade-unionism; freedom of religion without any discrimination; and the right of all patriotic organizations of whatever political tendency to carry on normal activities.

3. Proclaim a general amnesty for all political prisoners and the dissolution of concentration camps of all sorts; abolish fascist law 10/59 and all the other antidemocratic laws; authorize the return to the country of all persons persecuted by the American-Diem regime who are now refugees abroad.

4. Interdict all illegal arrests and detentions; prohibit torture; and punish all the Diem bullies who have not repented and who have committed crimes against the people.

III. *Establish an independent and sovereign economy, and improve the living conditions of the people.*

1. Suppress the monopolies imposed by the American imperialists and their servants; establish an independent and sovereign economy and finances in accordance with the national interest; confiscate to the profit of the nation the properties of the American imperialists and their servants.

2. Support the national bourgeoisie in the reconstruction and development of crafts and industry; provide active protection for national products through the suppression of

production taxes and the limitation or prohibition of imports that the national economy is capable of producing; reduce custom fees on raw materials and machines.

3. Revitalize agriculture; modernize production, fishing, and cattle raising; help the farmers in putting to the plow unused land and in developing production; protect the crops and guarantee their disposal.

4. Encourage and reinforce economic relations between the city and country, the plain and the mountain regions; develop commercial exchanges with foreign countries, regardless of their political regime, on the basis of equality and mutual interests.

5. Institute a just and rational system of taxation; eliminate harassing penalties.

6. Implement the labor code: prohibition of discharges, of penalties, of ill-treatment of wage earners; improvement of the living conditions of workers and civil servants; imposition of wage scales and protective measures for young apprentices.

7. Organize social welfare: find work for jobless persons; assume the support and protection of orphans, old people, invalids; come to the help of the victims of the Americans and Diemists; organize help for areas hit by bad crops, fires, or natural calamities.

8. Come to the help of displaced persons desiring to return to their native areas and to those who wish to remain permanently in the South; improve their working and living conditions.

9. Prohibit expulsions, spoliation, and compulsory concentration of the population; guarantee job security for the urban and rural working populations.

IV. Reduce land rent; implement agrarian reform with the aim of providing land to the tillers.

1. Reduce land rent; guarantee to the farmers the right to till the soil; guarantee the property right of accession to fallow lands to those who have cultivated them; guarantee property rights to those farmers who have already received land.

2. Dissolve 'prosperity zones' and put an end to recruit-

ment for the camps that are called 'agricultural development centers.' Allow those compatriots who already have been forced into 'prosperity zones' and 'agricultural development centers' to return freely to their own lands.

3. Confiscate the land owned by American imperialists and their servants, and distribute it to poor peasants without any land or with insufficient land; redistribute the communal lands on a just and rational basis.

4. By negotiation and on the basis of fair prices, repurchase for distribution to landless peasants or peasants with insufficient land those surplus lands that the owners of large estates will be made to relinquish if their domain exceeds a certain limit, to be determined in accordance with regional particularities. The farmers who benefit from such land and distribution will both be compelled to make any payment or to submit to any other conditions.

V. Develop a national and democratic culture and education.

1. Combat all forms of culture and education enslaved to Yankee fashions; develop a culture and education that is national, progressive, and at the service of the Fatherland and people.

2. Liquidate illiteracy; increase the number of schools in the fields of general education as well as in those of technical and professional education, in advanced study as well as in other fields; adopt Vietnamese as the vernacular language; reduce the expenses of education and exempt from payment students who are without means; resume the examination system.

3. Promote science and technology and the national letters and arts; encourage and support the intellectuals and artists so as to permit them to develop their talents in the service of national reconstruction.

4. Watch over public health; develop sports and physical education.

VI. Create a national army devoted to the defense of the Fatherland and the people.

1. Establish a national army devoted to the defense of

the Fatherland and the people; abolish the system of American military advisers.

2. Abolish the draft system, improve the living conditions of the simple soldiers and guarantee their political rights; put an end to ill-treatment of the military; pay particular attention to the dependents of soldiers without means.

3. Reward officers and soldiers having participated in the struggle against the domination by the Americans and their servants; adopt a policy of clemency toward the former collaborators of the Americans and Diemists guilty of crimes against the people but who have finally repented and are ready to serve the people.

4. Abolish all foreign military bases established on the territory of Viet-Nam.

VII. Guarantee equality between the various minorities and between the two sexes; protect the legitimate interest of foreign citizens established in Viet-Nam and of Vietnamese citizens residing abroad.

1. Implement the right to autonomy of the national minorities: Found autonomous zones in the areas with a minority population, those zones to be an integral part of the Vietnamese nation. Guarantee equality between the various nationalities: each nationality has the right to use and develop its language and writing system, to maintain or to modify freely its mores and customs; abolish the policy of the Americans and Diemists of racial discrimination and forced assimilation. Create conditions permitting the national minorities to reach the general level of progress of the population: development of their economy and culture; formation of cadres of minority nationalities.

2. Establish equality between the two sexes; women shall have equal rights with men from all viewpoints (political, economic, cultural, social, etc.).

3. Protect the legitimate interest of foreign citizens established in Viet-Nam.

4. Defend and take care of the interest of Vietnamese citizens residing abroad.

VIII. Promote a foreign policy of peace and neutrality.

1. Cancel all unequal treaties that infringe upon the sovereignty of the people and that were concluded with other countries by the servants of the Americans.

2. Establish diplomatic relations with all countries, regardless of their political regime, in accordance with the principles of peaceful coexistence adopted at the Bandung Conference.

3. Develop close solidarity with peace-loving nations and neutral countries; develop free relations with the nations of Southeast Asia, in particular with Cambodia and Laos.

4. Stay out of any military bloc; refuse any military alliance with another country.

5. Accept economic aid from any country willing to help us without attaching any conditions to such help.

IX. *Re-establish normal relations between the two zones, and prepare for the peaceful reunification of the country.*

The peaceful reunification of the country constitutes the dearest desire of all our compatriots throughout the country. The National Liberation Front of South Viet-Nam advocates the peaceful reunification by stages on the basis of negotiations and through the seeking of ways and means in conformity with the interest of the Vietnamese nation.

While awaiting this reunification, the governments of the two zones will, on the basis of negotiations, promise to banish all separatist and warmongering propaganda and not to use force to settle differences between the zones. Commercial and cultural exchanges between the two zones will be implemented and the inhabitants of the two zones will be free to move about throughout the country as their family and business interests indicate. The freedom of postal exchanges will be guaranteed.

X. *Struggle against all aggressive war; actively defend universal peace.*

1. Struggle against all aggressive war and against all forms of imperialist domination; support the national emancipation movements of the various peoples.

2. Banish all warmongering propaganda; demand general disarmament and the prohibition of nuclear weapons;

and advocate the utilization of atomic energy for peaceful purposes.

3. Support all movements of struggle for peace, democracy, and social progress throughout the world; contribute actively to the defense of peace in Southeast Asia and in the world.

Vietnam and the Domino Theory

John F. Kennedy

When the Second World War ended, most Americans thought of Vietnam as a relatively small and unimportant patch of land on the other side of the globe that was of little interest to the United States. In a series of speeches in 1953 and 1954, however, President Dwight Eisenhower laid out the case for American involvement, advancing what came to be known as the "Domino Theory." According to this theory, if even a single country in Southeast Asia fell to communism, it would rapidly lead to Communist domination of the entire region. In the following 1963 interview, President John F. Kennedy accepts the truth of the Domino Theory and says that the United States should not withdraw from Vietnam. Kennedy, a Democrat from Massachusetts, was president from 1961 until his assassination in 1963. He was interviewed by Chet Huntley and David Brinkley of *The Huntley-Brinkley Report*, a popular NBC news program from 1956 to 1970.

As you read, consider the following questions:
1. How does Kennedy respond to the claim that the U.S. government is occasionally locked into a position from which a change or shift is difficult?
2. Why does Kennedy think it would be unwise for the United States to reduce its aid to South Vietnam?
3. What challenges does Kennedy say the United States faces in exercising influence in Southeast Asia?

John F. Kennedy, *Public Papers of the Presidents of the United States*. Washington, DC: United States Government Printing Office, 1964.

Mr. Huntley: Mr. President, in respect to our difficulties in South Viet-Nam, could it be that our government tends occasionally to get locked into a policy or an attitude and then finds it difficult to alter or shift that policy?

PRESIDENT KENNEDY. Yes, that is true. I think in the case of South Viet-Nam we have been dealing with a government which is in control, has been in control for 10 years. In addition, we have felt for the last 2 years that the struggle against the Communists was going better. Since June [1963], however, the difficulties with the Buddhists [who were protesting the South Viet-Nam government], we have been concerned about a deterioration, particularly in the Saigon area, which hasn't been felt greatly in the outlying areas but may spread. So we are faced with the problem of wanting to protect the area against the Communists. On the other hand, we have to deal with the government there. That produces a kind of ambivalence in our efforts which exposes us to some criticism. We are using our influence to persuade the government there to take those steps which will win back support. That takes some time and we must be patient, we must persist.

Mr. Huntley: Are we likely to reduce our aid to South Viet-Nam now?

THE PRESIDENT. I don't think we think that would be helpful at this time. If you reduce your aid, it is possible you could have some effect upon the government structure there. On the other hand, you might have a situation which could bring about a collapse. Strongly in our mind is what happened in the case of China at the end of World War II, where China was lost, a weak government became increasingly unable to control events. We don't want that.

Mr. Brinkley: Mr. President, have you had any reason to doubt this so-called "domino theory," that if South Viet-Nam falls, the rest of southeast Asia will go behind it?

THE PRESIDENT. No, I believe it. I believe it. I think that the struggle is close enough. China is so large, looms so high just beyond the frontiers, that if South Viet-Nam went, it would not only give them an improved geographic position for a guerrilla assault on Malaya, but would also give the impression that the wave of the future in southeast Asia was China and the Communists. So I believe it. . . .

Mr. Brinkley: With so much of our prestige, money, so on, committed in South Viet-Nam, why can't we exercise a little more influence there, Mr. President?

THE PRESIDENT. We have some influence. We have some influence, and we are attempting to carry it out. I think we don't—we can't expect these countries to do every thing the way we want to do them. They have their own interest, their own personalities, their own tradition. We can't make everyone in our image, and there are a good many people who don't want to go in our image. In addition, we have ancient struggles between countries. In the case of India and Pakistan, we would like to have them settle Kashmir [a disputed area between India and Pakistan]. That is our view of the best way to defend the subcontinent against communism. But that struggle between India and Pakistan is more important to a good many people in that area than the struggle against the Communists. We would like to have Cambodia, Thailand, and South Viet-Nam all in harmony, but there are ancient differences there. We can't make the world over, but we can influence the world. The fact of the matter is that with the assistance of the United States, SEATO [South East Asia Treaty Organization], southeast Asia and indeed all of Asia has been maintained independent against a powerful force, the Chinese Communists. What I am concerned about is that Americans will get impatient and say because they don't like events in southeast Asia or they don't like the government in Saigon, that we should withdraw. That only makes it easy for the Communists. I think we should stay. We should use our influence in as effective a way as we can, but we should not withdraw.

2

THE ESCALATION
OF AMERICAN
INVOLVEMENT

CHAPTER PREFACE

In the early 1960s the American presence in South Vietnam deepened as the United States worked to prop up President Ngo Dinh Diem, who was struggling to hold onto power. Diem had never been popular, but his opponents began to resort to violence in the late 1950s after he effectively crushed political resistance through harsh laws and mass arrests of suspected Communists, dissident intellectuals, and unsympathetic journalists. Some of President John F. Kennedy's advisers recommended sending combat troops, but Kennedy chose instead to send military advisers and equipment to help Diem stabilize his government. Most in the Kennedy administration recognized that Diem was not an ideal leader, but they reasoned that he was the best in a set of bad options.

By 1963 sixteen thousand American military advisers were in South Vietnam, but it was becoming increasingly clear that the Diem presidency was doomed. In addition to Communist opponents, Diem faced serious protests from Buddhists, who had suffered religious discrimination under Diem, who was a Roman Catholic. When word reached Washington in the fall of 1963 that Diem's generals were planning a coup to overthrow the embattled leader the United States gave its quiet assent. Diem was deposed and executed in November 1963.

Lyndon Johnson, who became the American president after Kennedy was assassinated just a few weeks after the coup deposing Diem, adopted a more aggressive policy than had Kennedy. Like Kennedy and President Dwight Eisenhower before him, Johnson believed in the Domino Theory, which held that if South Vietnam fell to communism it would lead to Communist domination of all of Southeast Asia. After Vietnamese torpedo boats reportedly attacked an American ship patrolling in the Gulf of Tonkin in August 1964, Johnson pressed the U.S. Congress for a resolution giving him broad war powers. The Gulf of Tonkin Resolution, which passed unanimously in the House and with only two dissenting votes in the Senate, gave Johnson the authority to "take all necessary steps, including the use of armed force," to protect American forces in the region. This is the closest Congress came to declaring war on Vietnam.

Although there were some retaliatory air strikes against North Vietnam immediately after passage of the Gulf of Tonkin Resolution, the Johnson administration devoted the remainder of 1964 to debating American policy toward Vietnam. The Joint Chiefs of Staff advocated a wider air campaign against North Vietnam, but the civilians in the Pentagon favored limited bombings. After the National Liberation Front (NLF), an umbrella group of revolutionaries in South Vietnam, attacked two American army installations in South Vietnam in early 1965, however, Johnson ordered sustained bombing of North Vietnam. (Scholars debate the nature of the connection between the National Liberation Front and North Vietnam, but the U.S. government at the time believed that the NLF took its orders directly from North Vietnam.)

When the air campaign, dubbed Operation Rolling Thunder, commenced, and when U.S. combat troops arrived in Vietnam in March 1965, the leaders of the Communist Party of Vietnam reassessed their military strategy. They realized that they did not have the size or strength to take on the U.S. military in large-scale battles, so they shifted to a protracted war strategy. The new plan aimed to get the United States bogged down in a war that it did not want and that it could not effectively win. Eventually, the Communists hoped, the United States would withdraw from the war for political reasons. Although the United States halted its bombing campaign several times in 1965 in the hope that North Vietnam would negotiate, the American troop buildup continued, and by the end of the year there were 185,000 American troops in South Vietnam. The documents in this chapter explore the motivations behind this military escalation as well as various perspectives on America's actions in the region.

A Just Response to Unjust Attacks in the Gulf of Tonkin

Adlai E. Stevenson

In early August 1964 the United States accused North Vietnam of twice firing on U.S. Navy ships while they were in international waters in the Gulf of Tonkin, off the coast of North Vietnam. In the following statement presented to the United Nations Security Council on August 5 of that year, Adlai E. Stevenson gives the American side of the story. According to Stevenson, on August 2 the destroyer *Maddox* was attacked by three North Vietnamese torpedo boats, and on August 4 the *Maddox* and the *C. Turner Joy* were attacked by North Vietnamese torpedo boats. Stevenson also explains what he calls the "limited and measured" American response. The official American version of the Gulf of Tonkin incident was widely accepted in the United States and played a major role in getting Congress to approve the Gulf of Tonkin resolution, which authorized the president to "take all necessary measures" to prevent further aggression. Serious doubts were later raised, however, about the accuracy of the reports and about President Lyndon Johnson's knowledge of possible inaccuracy in them. In particular, critics charged that at the time of the first attack, the *Maddox* was engaged in aggressive intelligence-gathering operations and that it was thus misleading to describe the initial attack as "unprovoked." Furthermore, many now believe the report of the second attack was imaginary and that President Johnson knew so. Stevenson, who twice ran unsuccessfully for president on the Demo-

Adlai E. Stevenson, "Statement to the Security Council," *Department of State Bulletin*, August 24, 1964, pp. 272–74.

cratic ticket, was appointed U.S. ambassador to the United Nations in 1961 and served until his death in July 1965.

As you read, consider the following questions:
1. How did the United States respond to the reported hostilities?
2. Why does Stevenson think the American response is justified?
3. According to Stevenson, why is the United States involved in Vietnam?

I have asked for this urgent meeting to bring to the attention of the Security Council acts of deliberate aggression by the Hanoi regime against naval units of the United States.

Naval vessels of my Government, on routine operations in international waters in the Gulf of Tonkin, have been subjected to deliberate and repeated armed attacks. We, therefore, have found it necessary to take defensive measures.

The major facts about these incidents were announced last night by the President of the United States and communicated to other governments at the same time I was instructed to request this meeting. I shall recount these facts for you, Mr. President [of the Security Council], in chronological order so that all the members may have all the information available to my Government.

At 8:08 A.M. Greenwich meridian time, August 2, 1964, the United States destroyer *Maddox* was on routine patrol in international waters in the Gulf of Tonkin, proceeding in a southeasterly direction away from the coast about 30 miles at sea from the mainland of North Viet-Nam. The *Maddox* was approached by three high-speed North Vietnamese torpedo boats in attack formation. When it was evident that these torpedo boats intended to take offensive action, the *Maddox*, in accordance with naval practice, fired three warning shots across the bows of the approaching vessels. At approximately the same time, the aircraft carrier *Ticonderoga*, which was also in international waters and had been alerted to the impending attack, sent out four aircraft to provide cover for the *Maddox*, the pilots being under orders not to fire unless they or the *Maddox* were fired upon first.

Two of the attacking craft fired torpedoes, which the *Maddox* evaded by changing course. All three attacking vessels directed machinegun fire at the *Maddox*. One of the attacking vessels approached for close attack and was struck by fire from the *Maddox*. After the attack was broken off, the *Maddox* continued on a southerly course in international waters.

Now, Mr. President, clearly this was a deliberate armed attack against a naval unit of the United States Government on patrol in the high seas—almost 30 miles off the mainland. Nevertheless, my Government did its utmost to minimize the explosive potential of this flagrant attack in the hopes that this might be an isolated or uncalculated action. There was local defensive fire. The United States was not drawn into hasty response.

On August 3 the United States took steps to convey to the Hanoi regime a note calling attention to this aggression, stating that United States ships would continue to operate freely on the high seas in accordance with the rights guaranteed by international law, and warning the authorities in Hanoi of the "grave consequences which would inevitably result from any further unprovoked offensive military action against United States forces." This notification was in accordance with the provisions of the Geneva accords.

A Second Attack

Our hopes that this was an isolated incident did not last long. At 2:35 P.M. Greenwich meridian time, August 4, when it was nighttime in the Gulf of Tonkin, the destroyers *Maddox* and *C. Turner Joy* were again subjected to an armed attack by an undetermined number of motor torpedo boats of the North Vietnamese navy. This time the American vessels were 65 miles from shore, twice as far out on the high seas as on the occasion of the previous attack.

This time numerous torpedoes were fired. That attack lasted for over 2 hours.

There no longer could be any shadow of doubt that this was a planned, deliberate military aggression against vessels lawfully present in international waters. One could only conclude that this was the work of authorities dedicated to the use of force to achieve their objectives, regardless of the consequences.

My Government therefore determined to take positive but limited and relevant measures to secure its naval units against further aggression. Last night aerial strikes were thus carried out against North Vietnamese torpedo boats and their support facilities. This action was limited in scale, its only targets being the weapons and facilities against which we had been forced to defend ourselves. Our fervent hope is that the point has now been made that acts of armed aggression are not to be tolerated in the Gulf of Tonkin any more than they are to be tolerated anywhere else.

I want to emphasize that the action we have taken is a limited and measured response, fitted precisely to the attack that produced it, and that the deployments of additional U.S. forces to Southeast Asia are designed solely to deter further aggression. This is a single action designed to make unmistakably clear that the United States cannot be diverted by military attack from its obligations to help its friends establish and protect their independence. Our naval units are continuing their routine patrolling on the high seas with orders to protect themselves with all appropriate means against any further aggression. As President [Lyndon] Johnson said last night, "We still seek no wider war."

Mr. President, let me repeat that the United States vessels were in international waters when they were attacked.

Let me repeat that freedom of the seas is guaranteed under long-accepted international law applying to all nations alike.

Let me repeat that these vessels took no belligerent actions of any kind until they were subject to armed attack.

And let me say once more that the action they took in

self-defense is the right of all nations and is fully within the provisions of the Charter of the United Nations.

Part of a Pattern

The acts of aggression by the North Vietnamese in the Gulf of Tonkin make no sense whatsoever standing alone. They defy rational explanation except as part of a larger pattern with a larger purpose. As isolated events, the kidnapping of village officials in the Republic of South Viet-Nam makes no sense either. Neither does the burning of a schoolhouse—or the sabotage of an irrigation project—or the murder of a medical worker—or the random bomb thrown into a crowd of innocent people sitting in a cafe.

All these wanton acts of violence and destruction fit into the larger pattern of what has been going on in Southeast Asia for the past decade and a half. So does the arming of terrorist gangs in South Viet-Nam by the regimes in Hanoi and Peiping [Beijing]. So does the infiltration of armed personnel to make war against the legitimate government of that nation. So does the fighting in Laos—and all the acts of subversion—and all the propaganda—and the sabotage of the international machinery established to keep the peace by the Geneva agreements—and the deliberate, systematic, and flagrant violations of those agreements by two regimes which signed them and which by all tenets of decency, law, and civilized practice are bound by their provisions.

The attempt to sink United States destroyers in international waters is much more spectacular than the attempt to murder the mayor of a village in his bed at night. But they are both part of the pattern, and the pattern is designed to subjugate the people of Southeast Asia to an empire ruled by means of force of arms, of rule by terror, of expansion by violence.

Mr. President, it is only in this larger view that we can discuss intelligently the matter that we have brought to this Council.

In his statement last night, President Johnson concluded by emphasizing that the mission of the United States is peace. Under the explicit instructions of President Johnson, I want to repeat that assurance in the Security Council this afternoon: Our mission is peace.

We hoped that the peace settlement in 1954 would lead to peace in Viet-Nam. We hoped that that settlement, and the supplementary Geneva accords of 1962, would lead to peace in Laos. Communist governments have tried aggression before—and have failed. Each time the lesson has had to be learned anew.

We are dealing here with a regime that has not yet learned the lesson that aggression does not pay, cannot be sustained, and will always be thrown back by people who believe, as we do, that people want freedom and independence, not subjection and the role of satellite in a modern empire.

America's Goal in Asia
In Southeast Asia we want nothing more, and nothing less, than the assured and guaranteed independence of the peoples of the area. We are in Southeast Asia to help our friends preserve their own opportunity to be free of imported terror, alien assassination, managed by the North Viet-Nam Communists based in Hanoi and backed by the Chinese Communists from Peiping.

Two months ago, when we were discussing in this Council the problems created on the Cambodia–South Viet-Nam frontier by the Communist Viet Cong, I defined our peace aims in Southeast Asia. I repeat them today:

There is a very easy way to restore order in Southeast Asia. There is a very simple, safe way to bring about the end of United States military aid to the Republic of Viet-Nam.

Let all foreign troops withdraw from Laos. Let all states in that area make and abide by the simple decision to leave their neighbors alone. Stop the secret subversion of other people's independence. Stop the clandestine and illegal transit of national frontiers. Stop the export of revolution and the doctrine of violence. Stop the violations of the political agreements reached at Geneva for the future of Southeast Asia.

The people of Laos want to be left alone.

The people of Viet-Nam want to be left alone.

The people of Cambodia want to be left alone.

When their neighbors decide to leave them alone—as they must—there will be no fighting in Southeast Asia and no need for American advisers to leave their homes to help these people resist aggression. Any time that decision can be put in enforcible terms, my Government will be only too happy to put down the burden that we have been sharing with those determined to preserve their independence. Until such assurances are forthcoming, we shall stand for the independence of free peoples in Southeast Asia as we have elsewhere.

That is what I said to this Council in May. That is what I repeat to this Council in August.

When the political settlements freely negotiated at the conference tables in Geneva are enforced, the independence of Southeast Asia will be guaranteed. When the peace agreements reached long ago are made effective, peace will return to Southeast Asia and military power can be withdrawn.

U.S. Actions in the Gulf of Tonkin Are Provocative

Nikita Khrushchev

When the United States reported in early August 1964 that American ships in the Gulf of Tonkin had been twice attacked by North Vietnamese torpedo boats, Nikita Khrushchev, the Soviet leader, wrote a letter to President Lyndon Johnson. In that letter, reprinted below, Khrushchev expresses concern about the American version of events and raises a number of issues. The perspective of Khrushchev, leader of the powerful Communist Soviet Union, was important because the Gulf of Tonkin incident involved armed conflict between the Communist North Vietnamese and the anti-Communist Americans.

As you read, consider the following questions:
1. What does Khrushchev think the American ships in the Gulf of Tonkin represent, and why does he think this?
2. What do you think Khrushchev means when he asks President Johnson to "again and again weigh possible consequences"?
3. Who does Khrushchev think is responsible for the military tension in the Gulf of Tonkin?

Dear Mr. President: I deem it necessary to personally inform you about the concern that we feel in connection with the events unfolding in the Gulf of Tonkin.

From the very outset I want to mention that we know about these events solely from those statements which have been made these days in Washington, from the published

Nikita Khrushchev, *Letter from Chairman Khrushchev to President Johnson, August 5, 1964*, Department of State, Presidential Correspondence, Lot 77 D 163, August 5, 1964.

orders to the American armed forces, from the reports of the news agencies and also from the statement, just published, by the spokesman of the High Command of the Vietnamese People's Army concerning the incident on August 2 in the Gulf of Tonkin. We do not have other information as yet. One thing is indisputable, however, the situation there has sharply deteriorated and military conflicts are taking place near the coast of the Democratic Republic of Vietnam and the Chinese People's Republic, in which warships of the U.S. Navy are participating as well as military planes—based on American aircraft carriers. Also obvious is the seriousness of these developments—indeed, it is impossible to rule out that they may mushroom into such proportions and turn in such a way that it will be difficult to say where they will stop.

American Provocation

We do not know exactly now just what has happened there. But even irrespective of this the fact remains that the warships of the U.S. Navy have entered the Gulf which cuts deeply into the territories of the DRV [Democratic Republic of Vietnam, i.e., North Vietnam] and the CPR, [Chinese People's Republic] and that it is from these ships that fire was opened and aircraft are being launched which according to the latest reports, are making strikes against objectives on the territory of the DRV. Suffice it to look at the map to convince oneself that except the DRV and the CPR there are no other states the territories of which adjoin the Gulf of Tonkin and that, consequently, the very fact of introduction of American warships in that Gulf under any circumstances cannot be viewed in any other way but as a military demonstration, as a challenge to the states whose shores are washed by that Gulf.

With all frankness I must say that if these actions of American warships and air forces pursue the aim of strengthening somehow the position of the corrupt and rotten South Vietnamese regime which exists—and this is no secret to anyone—only because of the foreign support, then such actions will not achieve the given aim. But to increase the danger of a serious military conflict—they can.

An Ominous Shadow

A question arises before me: have not clouds been deliberately darkened around the developments in the Gulf of Tonkin? Is not the influence felt here by those quarters and persons who do not conceal their desire to inflame the passions, to pour oil on the flame and whose militant frame of mind one should regard with great caution and restraint? But if this influence is indeed real and if it has an ear, then another, more serious question arises—where the present developments can lead to?

It would be unnecessary to speak in detail now about the enormous responsibility which our two powers bear, you personally as President of the United States and I as Chairman of the U.S.S.R. Council of Ministers, in keeping the peace, in ensuring that dangerous events whichever area of the globe they begin with, would not become first elements in the chain of ever more critical and maybe irreversible events. I believe that you should agree with this. And if this is so, then at this moment it is most important to draw from this necessary practical conclusions and proceeding from this lofty responsibility to look at the circumstances around the developments in the Gulf of Tonkin with maximum objectivity and to again and again weigh possible consequences.

I would not like here to give play to feelings although this, in all appearance, is justified by the situation. Because of lack of reliable information I confine myself to expressing those thoughts which follow from the main and undeniable fact, namely, that the warships and air forces of the United States have taken military action in the Gulf of Tonkin area.

I want to emphasize that no one has asked the Soviet Government to address you in connection with the developments near the coast of the DRV and the CPR. If there appears a threat to peace, I am deeply convinced that we should not wait for requests or appeals from anybody but must act so as to remove that threat without delay.

I would like to hope that on your part there will be shown necessary composure and restraint in order to remove the military tension and stop defiant actions of the American armed forces in the Gulf of Tonkin area which may lead to an appropriate response from the other side.

Sincerely, N. Khrushchev

U.S. Policy in Vietnam Is Misguided

John Gange

In the following article, originally published in late August 1964 in the *Nation*, John Gange offers his interpretation of how and why the United States came to be deeply involved in Vietnam. According to Gange, the United States chose the course of action it did because it was relying on what Gange calls a mix of fact and myth. Gange is critical of American policy and argues that, as of 1964, American involvement in Vietnam is heading in a bad direction without any clear vision for the future. Gange was a former officer in the State Department and, at the time of writing, the director of the Institute of International Studies and Overseas Administration at the University of Oregon.

As you read, consider the following questions:
1. According to Gange, what two options did America face in 1954, and what did it decide to do?
2. What are the three "facts" and the three "myths" Gange says shaped American policy toward Vietnam?
3. What specific criticism does Gange have of the American course of action?

The weathered headstones in the old Protestant cemetery of Portuguese Macao tell of the misadventures of many Americans in the Gulf of Tonkin and the South China Sea. In the early years of our Republic, the Americans who died in this faraway area were sailors. Yankee traders, missionaries and visionary diplomats—like Edmund Roberts, who first

John Gange, "The Mix of Fact and Myth," *The Nation*, August 24, 1964, pp. 63–66. Copyright © 1964 by The Nation Magazine/The Nation Company, Inc. Reproduced by permission.

sought treaties for the United States in Southeast Asia, journeying to Cochin China, Siam and Muscat in 1832. Today, the headlines toll the death of many Americans pursuing the political interests of the United States in Southeast Asia.

From small beginnings our interest in Southeast Asia swelled to include a colonial empire highlighted by our half century in the Philippines. The United States blundered into empire in 1898 by deafeating the weak Spanish imperialists in the Battle of Manila Bay. Now we are fighting again in the Gulf of Tonkin and in the steaming jungles of old Indo-China. For many Americans today our deep involvement in Southeast Asia's civil wars is as inexplicable as was our plunge into empire in the Philippines. For fourteen years we have propped the French effort to keep Indo-China, or have underwritten the "democratic" regimes of such as Bao Dai, Ngo Dinh Diem and the subsequent military dictators. We have stumbled into "colonial" responsibilities without corresponding authority since the defeat of France by the Vietnamese in 1954.

The dilemma we faced in mid-1954 was very different in some respects from the dilemma President [William] McKinley faced in 1898 when he was informed that all of the Philippine Islands were ours for the taking—and holding. In 1954, there was nothing ready for the taking in Indo-China—unless we were prepared to battle the well-armed, well-led and tough Vietnamese and almost certainly the colossus of Communist China. We nevertheless decided to try to hold South Vietnam against a Communist take-over.

Underestimating Support for Communism

In doing so we underestimated Communist power and the response of great numbers of the Vietnamese to Ho Chi Minh's leadership, plus the extent of Communist outside aid, especially from the Chinese. When Secretary [of State John Foster] Dulles went to the Geneva Conference of April, 1954, called to discuss Korea and dispose of the pieces of the broken French empire in Indo-China, reportedly he refused to look at the chief Communist Chinese delegate, Premier Chou En-lai. This news sparked one of Fletcher Knebel's best quips to the effect that the Republicans were an odd lot, for Senator Joseph R. McCarthy saw Communists where they did not exist, and Secretary Dulles couldn't see them where they did exist. And here is a large part of our trouble: the refusal to look at facts which we dislike and hope will go away.

It has taken the French, through the voice of General [Charles] de Gaulle, to tell us that no settlement of any Asian problem is possible that doesn't take Communist China fully into account. The British recognized this fact in 1950 but they have not been so blunt in asserting its validity. Americans have not dealt with a strong unified China since 1842, when the British forced the opening of several Chinese ports to Western trade with various related privileges. In 1844, we got our treaty with China including trading rights and extraterritorial courts for our citizens in China. This period of wars with the West marked the end of a strong China for a hundred years. It is time we now adjusted ourselves to the fact of a new China. Is this hard to accept? Indeed it is, and for a long time we will no doubt fight this gross fact of our times. Eventually, it will have to be accepted and it must henceforth be included in the ingredients that shape our Asian policy.

The American Path

In 1954, we chose not to join in the Final Declaration of the Geneva Conference on Indo-China of July 21, 1954. (The United States made a unilateral statement, however, accepting the armistice agreements.) All the other nations (U.K., France, USSR, People's Republic of China, Laos, Cambodia and the People's Republic of Vietnam [North Vietnam]) at this conference, except the State of Vietnam (South Vietnam), accepted the agreements drawn there. South Vietnam, with our backing, refused to carry out the provisions of the 1954 Geneva agreement for elections in North and South Vietnam to form one government and instead set its course against the intent of this agreement.

South Vietnam refused to permit the elections, began its military build-up, and prepared for the inevitable war of Vietnamese against Vietnamese, with both sides drawing on outside aid to maintain the fight. From here on it is the old familiar story of who first violated the accords or the intent of the accords, etc., etc. The fact that we first refused to accept them puts both the U.S. and South Vietnam in a dubious role—in the objective light of history—a role our government has been diligent to gloss over. We refused to permit "free elections" in Vietnam because we were sure we would lose them.

When we found the 1954 Geneva agreements unacceptable to us, although acceptable to the other signatory nations, we had two broad alternatives open to us. One alternative was to reject the final conclusions of the conference, disregarding thereby the majority decision, and continue our own bilateral policy with South Vietnam. This we chose to do.

The second alternative was to seek a higher forum than the Geneva Conference nations. Resort to the United Nations through various possible approaches would have involved all who were concerned with peace and freedom, which we alleged were threatened in Indo-China. The UN supervised an election and a plebiscite on the restoration of the monarchy in wartorn Greece in 1946. The conditions were hardly worse in all Vietnam in 1954, or even 1956, when a general election was to be held in July of that year. To those who say that a UN-supervised election in Vietnam would not have been acceptable to North Vietnam and Communist China, one answer is that we never tried this course of action and hence we can't say what the response might have been. Instead we pressed for a Southeast Asian military security pact, which Secretary Dulles had urged in 1954.

The [President Dwight] Eisenhower administration had just swallowed the bitter pill of negotiating with Communist China and North Korea an armistice in the Korean War. The Republican campaign oratory of 1952 would have sounded hollow and mocking indeed if the Dullesian trumpets of "liberation from communism" had sounded another retreat on the "rollback" front. Some prominent Republicans had wanted our fighting forces to join the Indo-Chinese fray in early 1954, beside France, but the general in the Commander in Chief's chair had overruled that, as he had rejected any renewal of fighting in Korea above the 38th parallel. Nevertheless, Republican leaders knew from innumerable charges of their own what a powerful weapon the Democrats would have in our domestic politics if the Republican administration now "lost Indo-China." Ironically enough, as with mainland China allegedly "lost" by the Democrats, the United States never *had* Indo-China and couldn't have held it if we had tried. Therefore, another war in Asia was not a feasible political course for a U.S. administration, even one led by a five-star general.

Yet we did decide to try to "hold" at least part of Indo-China, namely, the new State of Vietnam below the 17th parallel. And so the newest phase of Western adventure in Indo-China began with that decision. We have been trying for ten years to prove it a sound one.

A Mix of Myth and Fact

In retrospect the foundations for our 1954 decision appear to be part fact and part myth—a fairly common "mix" in foreign as well as domestic policy decisions. The facts were that (1) Southeast Asia was a recognized target of Communist subversion and possible take-over; (2) many of the native occupants of the Indo-Chinese peninsula wanted no part of a future regime that might be dominated by Communist-oriented leaders. For religious, economic and political reasons many feared the kind of society they would have if Ho Chi Minh and others of his strong Communist belief became the new rulers of this war-weary part of Asia. The foreign businessmen, rubber planters and mine operators also, of course, feared the consequences of a Communist regime.

Moreover, the United States had become so conspicuously identified with the French in their struggle against Ho Chi Minh, albeit in the name of defense against international communism, that no further action by us now would mean that we, as well as the French, had gone down to defeat in another sector of the "containment" periphery of militant anti-communism.

So much for three quite substantial facts: a strong Communist drive for Southeast Asia; internal Indo-Chinese anti-Communist opinion; and the posture, or "face," of the U.S. if no further efforts were made to "save" Indo-China.

On the side of the myths that entered into our policy calculations, directly or indirectly, there was first the one, still often expressed, that it was possible to "draw a line" beyond which there would not be tolerated any expansion of Communist control. This appealing myth evokes images of a resolute U.S. cavalry stand at the pass, or *"ils ne passerant"* at Verdun in World War I, or a more sophisticated but still quite naive "containment-of-communism" concept. Thinking of communism as an *ideology* ought to make people chary of expounding on "drawing a line" to stop the spread of ideas. Interestingly, history provides no example of appealing *ideas* having been impeded effectively in their spread and adoption because of lines drawn on political maps.

The second myth that we embraced was that military action would be an acceptable substitute for basic political and social action. Again the lessons of the bitter and frustrating American experience in Nicaragua, Haiti and Santo Domingo in the years between World Wars I and II were passed over or rejected, if ever remembered. Military force—if sufficient in amount and ruthless enough in direction—*can* suppress rebellions, but rarely has it produced the reforms of conditions which lead men to join the ranks of rebellion. We ventured to combine some economic and technical aid with military support, but the rationale for military measures has prevailed increasingly as our efforts in Indo-China have persisted. The creation of SEATO [South East Asia Treaty Organization] in 1954 epitomizes this futile faith in military power to solve the problems of disorder in politically inchoate states desperately in need of *social* reform.

The third myth that we followed was the "domino" theory of the inevitable loss of all of Asia and a vital threat to our own continental security if any additional part of Asia came under Communist control. This theory was the delight of Sen. William Knowland, who trumpeted it in the Senate and across the land as if it had the infallibility of Newton's law of gravity. Even President [John F.] Kennedy repeated the arguments of the "domino" theory and few voices were raised to question its logic of inevitable, irresistible and sequential massive defeat once the first (additional) little domino fell against the bastions of our friends.

The domino theory overlooks the possibility of strong reaction by other nations at different points when they are confronted by new circumstances clearly threatening *their* security. The theory assumes that all powerful forces are on only one side, always moving *outward*, and it neglects the possibility of disruptive internal forces and counterforces moving against the presumed massive seismic wave set in motion by any little change of political status. It is a negative, fearful and mechanistic view of politics and man, but for those very reasons it finds countless advocates.

No End in Sight

So we took some facts and added some myths and came up with a decision—many times reaffirmed—to deny all Southeast Asia to communism, with military aid, and we created SEATO to do the job for us. Ten years later this queasy foundation of fact and myth finds us mired very deeply and sinking in more and more. After expending many billions of dollars and sacrificing hundreds of lives in combat or related services, after twistings and turnings of CIA undercover operations, with resulting changes of leaders in some of the states, there is still no end in sight.

What could we have done that we didn't do? If it had been possible for the Republicans to have done other-

wise—or for the Democrats to have altered that policy after they took over in 1961—one would like to think that
they would surely have done so. The losses of American
lives, the outpouring of many billions of taxpayers' dollars
and the strains on our friendship with many other nations
which have not seen the issues as we have seen them,
would not normally be called assets to any political party
seeking voter support. And so the American people have
been told over and over that there were—and still are—no
other alternatives but to stand on the 17th parallel (or well
south of it) and fight the devils (allegedly all from the
north) in the ancient battlegrounds of Indo-China. What
we have done is intervene in a third civil war in Asia; China
and Korea being the other two very costly interventions.

Until recently, too, we have lacked critical voices which,
while not acting as "the devil's advocate," would at least
ask if we are *sure* that what we are attempting is the only
possible alternative acceptable to our people. Like McKinley and the Philippines, the vast majority of the American
people in 1954 had only the vaguest notion of where Laos,
Cambodia and Vietnam were—and they cared less. Do
they even now believe these areas so vital to their welfare
that very extensive and long-term involvement is all that
we can consider?

In due time, probably later than would have been an op-
timum time for us, we will be forced to face the "unthink-
able" possibility of the neutralization of all of the Indo-
Chinese peninsula. Secretary of State [Dean] Rusk and
Secretary of Defense [Robert] McNamara repeatedly say
that no thought is being given to this alternative to our present massive military aid-*cum*-cheers-for-Khanh [the general who became prime minister of South Vietnam in 1964
after a coup] as our approach to the problem. The McNamara shuttle to Saigon carries threadbare calls for "greater
resolve" and warnings of "an unforseeable end to the effort," and then the familiar and unconvincing reports of
"gratifying progress" and "encouraging developments" on
the Westbound run back to Washington. In the meantime,

the Vietcong strike villages and cities at will in South Vietnam and simultaneously detail spare forces to push their campaign in Laos. Recruits and military equipment are picked up in abundance from the South Vietnamese civilian and military forces.

No Clear Plan

"Why are we involved in Southeast Asia?" "Where do we go for the next ten years?" These are the questions that beg and receive no clear answers, other than "Carry on! What was valid in 1954 is still valid in 1964" although the Asian world has changed greatly since then. At some point—and soon perhaps—we must face up to: (1) our dubious legal position in South Vietnam, with our shooting and destroying of military forces under the thin deceit of being "advisers"; (2) the soundness of our continuing passivity toward a strong role for the UN in Southeast Asian strife, while at the same time we have pressed for UN action in the internecine fighting of the Congo, Cyprus and the Middle East; (3) a new look at neutralization of "border" areas between East and West in Asia and the established examples, both satisfactory and unsatisfactory, of neutralization in Europe and elsewhere; (4) a hard review of all our interests in Asia, eventually in conference with Communist China; and (5) abandoning the shibboleth of containing communism along artificial latitudes or longitudes. The truth is that the ideological appeal of Marxist doctrine and the reforms that communism often has espoused effectively appeal to many people around the world; and the spread of these ideas will not be stopped by military fiat. Nor will it help at all to continue the repeated plaintive lament of Secretary Rusk that there would be peace in Indo-China if only the North Vietnamese and the Chinese would leave their neighbors alone. If all countries would leave their neighbors alone, it would be a very different world, but it is not realistic to expect this change in our times. To expand the war would assure only another Korea or worse, with all the possibilities of a nuclear war.

Will the new year or the post-election period see us re-examine our decade of "active defense" in Southeast Asia's Indo-Chinese peninsula? Perhaps not; it has become a habit to argue as we have for so long. Apparently only a Senator Wayne Morse can change his mind as fully as the circumstances require and still retain his following. Politics doesn't stop at the water's edge, but rather it governs all we do. Only a statesman above politics can change our course now. Events in Indo-China may not wait for our politicians to clear the November election hurdle before they can "lead" our discontented people to a new and more realistic settlement in Southeast Asia, and extricate us from a misadventure born of good motives based on some faulty calculations and expectations.

The President Needs to Address the Public and the Press

James Greenfield

American military action in Vietnam increased after the Gulf of Tonkin incident, and by early 1965 air strikes against North Vietnam were being conducted on a regular basis. In the following confidential memorandum to Secretary of State Dean Rusk, Assistant Secretary of State for Public Affairs James Greenfield discusses the American public's view of the military action in Vietnam. According to Greenfield, the Johnson administration faces two distinct public relations problems. Following his tenure as assistant secretary of state, Greenfield worked as foreign editor for the *New York Times* from 1969 until 1977.

As you read, consider the following questions:
1. Why does Greenfield think the president or the secretary of state should make a public statement?
2. How does Greenfield characterize the questions asked by the media, and what does he say about the answers to those questions?

The public problem on Viet-Nam currently breaks down into two problems: One, the need for some public statement, either on a Presidential or Secretarial level, that reiterates the United States stake in Viet-Nam and sets the tone for public discussion in this country. Two, the more intricate, detailed and searching investigation by the press of fu-

James Greenfield, *Viet Nam and the Public: Memorandum from the Assistant Secretary of State for Public Affairs to Secretary of State Rusk*, Department of State, Central Files, POL 27 VIET S, February 16, 1965.

ture U.S. aims and actions. These questions are both legitimate and pressing, but at the moment they reflect journalistic rather than public pressure.

Within government the tendency so far is to brush aside the general public statement on the excuse that it cannot include all the details demanded by the press. This argument is not valid.

The Public Statement

A public statement, either Presidential or on a high State Department level, should spell out some of the guidelines which will motivate our future actions in Viet-Nam. But this look into the future need not form the bulk of such a statement.

Instead, the statement should be dominated by a simple, direct restatement of U.S. policy. This restatement should outline the reasons why we are in South Viet-Nam, the nature of guerrilla warfare, the importance of the Pacific area to the United States, the alternatives that the U.S. faces and the consequences for both the U.S. and the free world that would occur if the United States did not carry out its commitment in Asia.

To people dealing closely with the problem this is old-hat, even boring stuff. But it would not be to the American public.

The argument that we have said all this before—and therefore should not repeat ourselves—is equally invalid. The rationale for our actions during the past few weeks was almost entirely dropped from most of the stories that appeared after the first day of bombings. In ninety percent of the stories, the reasons for our actions fell victim to the more dramatic factual news of bombings, Americans wounded, statements, threats and counter threats.

People, I am convinced, have lost sight of many of the past statements (and bits of statements) made in the past on Viet-Nam by the President and the Secretary. Our own two White House statements in the last ten days shifted emphasis without explanation. Almost no one remembers what the accords of 1954 and 1962 were all about, the rationale upon which they were based, or their applicability to the present situation.

Someone, therefore, should take them back through the essentials of our policy—back through the accords, back through our mounting involvement as this new kind of warfare unfolded, back through our countless statements that we want no bases and no territory for ourselves. We should remind the public that a free Viet-Nam is worth the risks, both because of our obligations to the Vietnamese and to ourselves.

It is not enough simply to say that we are in Viet-Nam because Ike [President Dwight Eisenhower] got us there or because the Vietnamese have asked us in, although both facts should be recalled.

Such a statement should end up by a clear declaration that what we seek is peace and as clear a statement as possible as to what we expect from the other side in order to gain that peace.

Such a statement will reassure the country, give it a common starting point to judge future U.S. actions.

The Questions of the Press

It will not, however, satisfy many of the questions being asked by the press such as those listed below. Many of them are currently unanswerable.

1. What is our objective in bombing the North?

—Is it unconditional surrender?

—Is it to drive the Viet Cong out of South Viet-Nam?

—Is it a cease-fire?

—Is it negotiations: if so with whom, what conditions, how arranged?

2. Why do we think the Viet Cong will give up if we bomb the North?

(Granted they are supplied and directed from Hanoi, but we acknowledge they have a strong local base and large measure of independence.)

3. Under what circumstances will we continue to bomb the North?

—only if major attacks on U.S. facilities continue? (i.e., tit-for-tat: theme of February 8 statement)

—at our discretion irrespective of specific attacks on U.S. personnel or installations? (White House statement of February 11)

4. What are we doing to prevent situation from returning to wasting guerrilla war that we haven't been able to win, with continuation of political instability in Saigon?

5. Any efforts going on to edge confrontation onto political track? What are circumstances under which we would talk to Hanoi, to Peiking [an alternative spelling of Peking, the former name for Beijing], to South Viet-Nam National Liberation Front and/or Viet Cong leadership?

If we won't talk do we have any objective other than complete withdrawal of Viet Cong to north of 17th Parallel?

Either the President or you [Secretary of State Dean Rusk] should make a statement setting forth the fundamentals of our position and relating recent events to those fundamentals. If you hold a press conference you must be prepared to open with a full statement on Viet-Nam, since many of the questions you will get are unanswerable—or better left unanswered.

The United States Does Not Belong in Vietnam

Mike Mansfield

In the following letter sent to President Lyndon Johnson in late March 1965, Senator Mike Mansfield expresses concern about American action in Vietnam and urges the president to reconsider America's deepening involvement. Mansfield, a senator from Montana, was considered an authority on U.S.-Asia relations and undertook foreign policy assignments for Presidents Franklin D. Roosevelt, John F. Kennedy, Lyndon Johnson, Richard Nixon, and Gerald Ford.

As you read, consider the following questions:
1. What concerns does Mansfield say he has raised to President Johnson over the years in regard to Vietnam?
2. What problems does Mansfield foresee American policy toward Vietnam leading to?
3. What effect does Mansfield think American involvement in Vietnam will have on Chinese influence in South Asia?

Dear Mr. President:

Over the years, I have submitted both to your predecessor and to you a series of memorandums on the situation in Viet Nam and Southeast Asia. Sometimes suggestions have been requested of me and sometimes they have been volunteered. In either case, they have been motivated solely by a desire to give such help as I might in the burdens of the decisions of the Presidency.

The main lines of thought in these memorandums over the years, as you may recall, are the following:

Mike Mansfield, *Letter to President Johnson, March 24, 1965*, Johnson Library, White House Central Files, EX ND 19/CO 312, March 24, 1965.

1. That the United States does not have interests on the Southeast Asian mainland to justify the costs in American lives and resources which would be required if we were to attempt to exercise, in effect, primacy over what transpires in that region; and that, insofar as South Viet Nam is concerned, we are there, not to take primary responsibility, but to provide whatever assistance is wanted and can be used effectively by the Vietnamese themselves.

2. That our national interest lies in reducing, rather than in increasing, the unilateral role which we have played in recent years, through the foreign aid program and excessive involvement of various United States agencies in the internal affairs of the weak nations of that region.

3. That our national security interests are best served in Southeast Asia by severely limiting our military involvement and, confining ourselves at most, to a very judicious use of air and sea power.

4. That the best prospects for a tolerable long-range situation in Southeast Asia lie in encouraging, through astute diplomacy and limited and preferably multilateral economic assistance, the emergence of truly independent governments with firm roots in their own people, which are as free as possible from great power involvement in their internal affairs. This situation, as I have noted, time and again, has prevailed in Cambodia at least until very recently when, in my judgment, a combination of years of inept diplomacy and the events in Viet Nam finally conspired to push this small and ably-led nation sharply towards China. It has prevailed to some extent in Burma and at one time, there was hope for it in South Viet Nam under the late Ngo Dinh Diem.

I am aware that the principles of policy outlined in the four points above are subject to the charge of "a return to isolationism." It should be noted, however, that there is no automatic virtue in an ubiquitous and indiscriminate internationalism, particularly when it leads to the kind of isolated internationalism in which we presently find ourselves in Viet Nam.

A Different Direction

I think it is correct to say that the trend of our policies over the past few years has been in a direction opposite to the main lines of thought which are contained in my memorandums over the past few years. I say this, as you know, without rancor or criticism. I know that my thoughts have received your careful attention. I know that your assistants and the bureaucracy have studied them and occasionally even have concurred in an idea expressed in them.

Nevertheless, it is still a fact that present policy is on a course which contains the following diametric opposites of the suggestions which I have advanced over the years. Present policy, so far as I can determine, requires:

1. That we make whatever expenditure of American lives and resources, on an ascending scale, is necessary in order for us to exercise, in effect, a primacy over what transpires in South Viet Nam. If this involves going into North Viet Nam and beyond, that, too, will be done.

2. That in the absence of unconditional capitulation of the Viet Cong, our military involvement must continue and be increased as necessary (there is discussion even now of a Joint Command which can only be the prelude to United States command in fact if not in word).

3. That our military involvement will not be restricted to a most judicious use of air and sea power, as evidenced by instructions to strike at "targets of convenience," but rather that it be extended, even to the infusion of a steadily increasing number of American combat forces on the ground.

4. That we will not try to encourage, through sustained diplomatic efforts, the emergence of the kind of situations which exist in Burma and Cambodia, but rather, so far as I can see, that we will stress those situations which can be maintained only by continuous infusions of American aid (i.e., Laos and Thailand, not to speak of South Viet Nam itself).

Those are the facts of our policy as it is being carried out, as I see it. It is possible that this direction may not be precisely the one you seek, a possibility suggested by your calling to my attention this morning your unawareness in advance of the usage of gas in Viet Nam. It may be that you were also unaware in advance, understandably, of the usage of napalm and of the concept of "targets of convenience" which are likely to do at least as much damage to non-combatants as combatants in a situation such as Viet Nam or the countless other decisions which deepen our involvement and responsibility. May I say in connection with the gas that it is beyond my comprehension how any American in an office of responsibility would not realize the vast significance, beyond immediate military considerations, of this act and, therefore, seek the highest political authority before taking such a step.

It is this possibility, that actions of the bureaucracy may have taken us in more deeply than desired, which leads me to write you once again, and most respectfully suggest certain changes at this time which may move us from the present direction of policy as it is expressed in action. In all frankness, I believe that the present direction is at variance with the extent and nature of our national interests on the Southeast Asian mainland and in the world. In the end, I fear that this course, at best, will win us only more widespread difficulties which will play havoc with the domestic program of the Administration, with the balance of payments situation, and with our interests and constructive influence elsewhere in the world.

Suggestions for the President

I have no great hope that, at this late date, these suggestions will be useful to you. But for what they may be worth, I would suggest:

1. That we should concentrate any ground forces which are sent to Viet Nam to safeguard Americans already there in two or three key spots which either back up on the sea or are easily accessible from the sea (i.e.,

Saigon and Da Nang) and that all other Americans in Viet Nam should be drawn into these protected points as rapidly as possible. From the point of view of our diplomatic position, two or three accessible and more defensible bases will be of greater value than numerous installations in the interior which can become, one by one, the targets of massed Viet Cong attacks;

2. That we should seek, indirectly but forcefully, through all possible sources, a reconvening of the 1961 Geneva Conference group;

3. That we should insist upon, as the sole precondition for such a meeting, a total cease-fire and stand-fast throughout all of Viet Nam, north and south;

4. That we should be prepared for consultation between the Saigon government, the North Vietnamese and the opposition in the south on the conditions for maintaining the "ceasefire" and "stand-fast," and on subsequent relationships once a conference has been convened and, further, that we accept, if circumstances indicate the desirability of it, United Nations participation in this connection.

As you well know, it is very difficult to predict the evolution of a course of policy once it has been set in motion. There will be risks to our national interests in a conference, but certainly, in my opinion, risks which are far smaller than those which we now run. I think it should be pointed out that if there is a settlement it is possible that Chinese influence in Southeast Asia may increase, but that possibility is even greater if the present course is pursued further. A settlement would not necessarily mean, however, that China will automatically control the area in a military or even an economic sense. The historic counterforce to that domination is the general Southeast Asian fear and anxiety of the Chinese which is quite distinct and may be at least as strong as ideology. In present circumstances, this fear and anxiety would appear to be largely dormant but it could revive in the event of a Chinese attempt at subversion of subjugation, particularly after a settlement. The existing Sino-

Soviet dispute is also likely to distract China from Southeast Asia to some degree, but not in the event of a deepening military confrontation in that area.

I have written frankly and at length out of a deep concern over the present trend of events in Viet Nam. We are in very deep already and in most unfavorable circumstances. In my judgment we were in too deep long before you assumed office. But you know the whole situation on a day-to-day basis and I most certainly respect the decisions which you have felt compelled to make in this connection.

I shall not trouble you further with memorandums on this situation and I do not expect an answer to this letter. Your responsibilities are great and to what I have written, I know you must add the views of many others who see this situation in different terms. But I did want to put certain possibilities before you in the event you have not yet had an opportunity to explore them. And I want you to know that you have my support on a personal as well as an official basis. If there is anything I can do to help you in this as in any other matter you have only to ask and I will try to the best of my ability to do so.

Respectfully yours,
Mike Mansfield

The United States Will Prevail in Vietnam

Lyndon Johnson

In March 1965, the United States launched Operation Rolling Thunder, in which bombing sorties targeted North Vietnam, particularly near the border with South Vietnam. These were the first strikes against North Vietnam that were not directly in response to Communist aggression; as such, they were a clear sign of America's deepening involvement. In an important speech at Johns Hopkins University in Baltimore on April 7, 1965, Lyndon Johnson set forth the American position and pledged the United States would never leave Vietnam in defeat. Two weeks after his speech, Johnson raised American combat strength in Vietnam to more than 60,000 soldiers, and by the end of the year nearly 200,000 American troops were in Vietnam.

As you read, consider the following questions:
1. According to Johnson, why is the United States at war?
2. What are America's goals, according to Johnson?
3. What incentives for negotiation does Johnson offer North Vietnam?

I have come here to review once again with my own people the views of the American Government.

Tonight Americans and Asians are dying for a world where each people may choose its own path to change.

This is the principle for which our ancestors fought in the valleys of Pennsylvania. It is the principle for which our sons fight tonight in the jungles of Viet-Nam.

Lyndon B. Johnson, address at Johns Hopkins University, Baltimore, MD, April 7, 1965.

Viet-Nam is far away from this quiet campus. We have no territory there, nor do we seek any. The war is dirty and brutal and difficult. And some 400 young men, born into an America that is bursting with opportunity and promise, have ended their lives on Viet-Nam's steaming soil.

Why must we take this painful road?

Why must this Nation hazard its case, and its interest, and its power for the sake of a people so far away?

We fight because we must fight if we are to live in a world where every country can shape its own destiny. And only in such a world will our own freedom be finally secure.

This kind of world will never be built by bombs or bullets. Yet the infirmities of man are such that force must often precede reason, and the waste of war, the works of peace.

We wish that this were not so. But we must deal with the world as it is, if it is ever to be as we wish.

The Nature of the Conflict

The world as it is in Asia is not a serene or peaceful place.

The first reality is that North Viet-Nam has attacked the independent nation of South Viet-Nam. Its object is total conquest.

Of course, some of the people of South Viet-Nam are participating in attack on their own government. But trained men and supplies, orders and arms, flow in a constant stream from north to south.

This support is the heartbeat of the war.

And it is a war of unparalleled brutality. Simple farmers are the targets of assassination and kidnapping. Women and children are strangled in the night because their men are loyal to their government. And helpless villages are ravaged by sneak attacks. Large-scale raids are conducted on towns, and terror strikes in the heart of cities.

The confused nature of this conflict cannot mask the fact that it is the new face of an old enemy.

Over this war—and all Asia—is another reality: the deepening shadow of Communist China. The rulers in Hanoi are urged on by Peking. This is a regime which has destroyed freedom in Tibet, which has attacked India, and has been condemned by the United Nations for aggression in Korea. It is a nation which is helping the forces of violence in almost every continent. The contest in Viet-Nam is part of a wider pattern of aggressive purposes.

Why America Fights

Why are these realities our concern? Why are we in South Viet-Nam?

We are there because we have a promise to keep. Since 1954 every American President has offered support to the people of South Viet-Nam. We have helped to build, and we have helped to defend. Thus, over many years, we have made a national pledge to help South Viet-Nam defend its independence.

And I intend to keep that promise.

To dishonor that pledge, to abandon this small and brave nation to its enemies, and to the terror that must follow, would be an unforgivable wrong.

We are also there to strengthen world order. Around the globe, from Berlin to Thailand, are people whose well-being rests, in part, on the belief that they can count on us if they are attacked. To leave Viet-Nam to its fate would shake the confidence of all these people in the value of an American commitment and in the value of America's word. The result would be increased unrest and instability, and even wider war.

We are also there because there are great stakes in the balance. Let no one think for a moment that retreat from Viet-Nam would bring an end to conflict. The battle would be renewed in one country and then another. The central lesson of our time is that the appetite of aggression is never satisfied. To withdraw from one battlefield means only to prepare for the next. We must say in southeast Asia—as we did in Europe—in the words of the Bible: "Hitherto shalt thou come, but no further."

There are those who say that all our effort there will be futile—that China's power is such that it is bound to dominate all southeast Asia. But there is no end to that argument until all of the nations of Asia are swallowed up.

There are those who wonder why we have a responsibility there. Well, we have it there for the same reason that we have a responsibility for the defense of Europe. World War II was fought in both Europe and Asia, and when it ended we found ourselves with continued responsibility for the defense of freedom.

America's Goals

Our objective is the independence of South Viet-Nam, and its freedom from attack. We want nothing for ourselves—only that the people of South Viet-Nam be allowed to guide their own country in their own way.

We will do everything necessary to reach that objective. And we will do only what is absolutely necessary.

In recent months attacks on South Viet-Nam were stepped up. Thus, it became necessary for us to increase our response and to make attacks by air. This is not a change of purpose. It is a change in what we believe that purpose requires.

We do this in order to slow down aggression.

We do this to increase the confidence of the brave people of South Viet-Nam who have bravely borne this brutal battle for so many years with so many casualties.

And we do this to convince the leaders of North Viet-Nam—and all who seek to share their conquest—of a very simple fact:

We will not be defeated.

We will not grow tired.

We will not withdraw, either openly or under the cloak of a meaningless agreement.

We know that air attacks alone will not accomplish all of these purposes. But it is our best and prayerful, judgment that they are a necessary part of the surest road to peace.

We hope that peace will come swiftly. But that is in the hands of others besides ourselves. And we must be prepared for a long continued conflict. It will require patience as well as bravery, the will to endure as well as the will to resist.

I wish it were possible to convince others with words of what we now find it necessary to say with guns and planes: Armed hostility is futile. Our resources are equal to any challenge. Because we fight for values and we fight for principles, rather than territory or colonies, our patience and our determination are unending.

Once this is clear, then it should also be clear that the only path for reasonable men is the path of peaceful settlement.

Such peace demands an independent South Viet-Nam—securely guaranteed and able to shape its own relationships to all others—free from outside interference—tied to no alliance—a military base for no other country.

These are the essentials of any final settlement.

We will never be second in the search for such a peaceful settlement in Viet-Nam.

There may be many ways to this kind of peace: in discussion or negotiation with the governments concerned; in large groups or in small ones; in the reaffirmation of old agreements or their strengthening with new ones.

We have stated this position over and over again, fifty times and more, to friend and foe alike. And we remain ready, with this purpose, for unconditional discussions.

And until that bright and necessary day of peace we will try to keep conflict from spreading. We have no desire to see thousands die in battle—Asians or Americans. We have no desire to devastate that which the people of North Viet-Nam have built with toil and sacrifice. We will use our power with restraint and with all the wisdom that we can command.

But we will use it.

This war, like most wars, is filled with terrible irony. For what do the people of North Viet-Nam want? They want what their neighbors also desire: food for their hunger; health for their bodies; a chance to learn; progress for their country; and an end to the bondage of material misery. And they would find all these things far more readily in peaceful association with others than in the endless course of battle.

A Generous America

These countries of southeast Asia are homes for millions of impoverished people. Each day these people rise at dawn and struggle through until the night to wrestle existence from the soil. They are often wracked by disease, plagued by hunger, and death comes at the early age of 40.

Stability and peace do not come easily in such a land. Neither independence nor human dignity will ever be won, though, by arms alone. It also requires the work of peace. The American people have helped generously in times past in these works. Now there must be a much more massive effort to improve the life of man in that conflict-torn corner of our world.

The first step is for the countries of southeast Asia to associate themselves in a greatly expanded cooperative effort for development. We would hope that North Viet-Nam would take its place in the common effort just as soon as peaceful cooperation is possible.

The United Nations is already actively engaged in development in this area. As far back as 1961 I conferred with our authorities in Viet-Nam in connection with their work there. And I would hope tonight that the Secretary General of the United Nations could use the prestige of his great office, and his deep knowledge of Asia, to initiate, as soon as possible, with the countries of that area, a plan for cooperation in increased development.

For our part I will ask the Congress to join in a billion dollar American investment in this effort as soon as it is underway.

And I would hope that all other industrialized countries, including the Soviet Union, will join in this effort to replace despair with hope, and terror with progress.

The task is nothing less than to enrich the hopes and the existence of more than a hundred million people. And there is much to be done.

The vast Mekong River can provide food and water and power on a scale to dwarf even our own TVA [Tennessee Valley Authority, the largest American public power company].

The wonders of modern medicine can be spread through villages where thousands die every year from lack of care.

Schools can be established to train people in the skills that are needed to manage the process of development.

And these objectives, and more, are within the reach of a cooperative and determined effort.

I also intend to expand and speed up a program to make available our farm surpluses to assist in feeding and clothing the needy in Asia. We should not allow people to go hungry and wear rags while our own warehouses overflow with an abundance of wheat and corn, rice and cotton.

So I will very shortly name a special team of outstanding, patriotic, distinguished Americans to inaugurate our participation in these programs. This team will be headed by Mr. Eugene Black, the very able former President of the World Bank.

In areas that are still ripped by conflict, of course development will not be easy. Peace will be necessary for final success. But we cannot and must not wait for peace to begin this job.

The Dream of World Order

This will be a disorderly planet for a long time. In Asia, as elsewhere, the forces of the modern world are shaking old ways and uprooting ancient civilizations. There will be turbulence and struggle and even violence. Great social change—as we see in our own country now—does not always come without conflict.

We must also expect that nations will on occasion be in dispute with us. It may be because we are rich, or powerful; or because we have made some mistakes; or because they honestly fear our intentions. However, no nation need ever fear that we desire their land, or to impose our will, or to dictate their institutions.

But we will always oppose the effort of one nation to conquer another nation.

We will do this because our own security is at stake.

But there is more to it than that. For our generation has a dream. It is a very old dream. But we have the power and now we have the opportunity to make that dream come true.

For centuries nations have struggled among each other. But we dream of a world where disputes are settled by law and reason. And we will try to make it so.

For most of history men have hated and killed one another in battle. But we dream of an end to war. And we will try to make it so.

For all existence most men have lived in poverty, threatened by hunger. But we dream of a world where all are fed and charged with hope. And we will help to make it so.

The ordinary men and women of North Viet-Nam and South Viet-Nam—of China and India—of Russia and America—are brave people. They are filled with the same proportions of hate and fear, of love and hope. Most of them want the same things for themselves and their families. Most of them do not want their sons to ever die in battle, or to see their homes, or the homes of others, destroyed.

Well, this can be their world yet. Man now has the knowledge—always before denied—to make this planet serve the real needs of the people who live on it.

I know this will not be easy. I know how difficult it is for reason to guide passion, and love to master hate. The complexities of this world do not bow easily to pure and consistent answers.

But the simple truths are there just the same. We must all try to follow them as best we can.

We often say how impressive power is. But I do not find it impressive at all. The guns and the bombs, the rockets and the warships, are all symbols of human failure. They are necessary symbols. They protect what we cherish. But they are witness to human folly.

A dam built across a great river is impressive.

In the countryside where I was born, and where I live, I

have seen the night illuminated, and the kitchens warmed, and the homes heated, where once the cheerless night and the ceaseless cold held sway. And all this happened because electricity came to our area along the humming wires of the REA [Rural Electrification Administration, a government program to bring electricity to rural areas]. Electrification of the countryside—yes, that, too, is impressive.

A rich harvest in a hungry land is impressive.

The sight of healthy children in a classroom is impressive.

These—not mighty arms—are the achievements which the American Nation believes to be impressive.

And, if we are steadfast, the time may come when all other nations will also find it so.

Every night before I turn out the lights to sleep I ask myself this question: Have I done everything that I can do to unite this country? Have I done everything I can to help unite the world, to try to bring peace and hope to all the peoples of the world? Have I done enough?

Ask yourselves that question in your homes—and in this hall tonight. Have we, each of us, all done all we could? Have we done enough?

We may well be living in the time foretold many years ago when it was said: "I call heaven and earth to record this day against you, that I have set before you life and death, blessing and cursing: therefore choose life, that both thou and thy seed may live."

This generation of the world must choose: destroy or build, kill or aid, hate or understand.

We can do all these things on a scale never dreamed of before.

Well, we will choose life. In so doing we will prevail over the enemies within man, and over the natural enemies of all mankind.

3

THE FACE OF WAR

CHAPTER PREFACE

The Vietnam War was a different kind of war, at least for the United States. American generals had studied and in many cases experienced World War II, in which opposing armies met on battlefields to fight for control of territory. In Vietnam, however, there was no "front" between the American and South Vietnamese forces and their opponents. Rather, the enemy they faced moved secretly through the jungle, advancing to attack American and South Vietnamese positions and then retreating back into the jungle. It consisted of the North Vietnamese Army (NVA) and the Vietcong, a derisive term meaning "Vietnamese Communist," a guerrilla army within South Vietnam composed of those opposed to the South Vietnamese government.

In most traditional wars, military objectives focused on winning territory from the enemy and victory consisted in controlling all the territory. The advance, attack, and retreat strategy employed by the NVA and the Vietcong, however, made the control of territory a largely meaningless goal for the United States to adopt in Vietnam. Consequently, American military objectives came to revolve around the "kill ratio," the percentage of American versus enemy casualties, with U.S. and South Vietnamese troops undertaking search-and-destroy missions intended to root out and kill NVA and Vietcong troops. Although the kill ratios tended to heavily favor the Americans, there seemed to be no end to the number of NVA and Vietcong troops who were prepared to make the ultimate sacrifice for the cause they believed in. In time, despite the favorable kill ratios, American casualties mounted. By the end of the war over fifty-eight thousand American service personnel had been killed.

For the young American soldiers, many of whom were draftees, life in the jungle was nightmarish. The environment itself was strange and new, and conditions were harsh, with heat and humidity taking a toll on morale. Furthermore, the search-and-destroy missions were dangerous since the troops conducting them were subject to ambushes and booby traps from an enemy that used the dense jungle to its advantage. Finally, because the Vietcong was not a regular army dressed in military uniforms and arranged in battlefield positions, it was very hard at times for American troops to distinguish between combatants and noncombatants.

Of the many battles and skirmishes during the Vietnam War, three stand out as especially significant. In January 1968 the NVA and the Vietcong launched a coordinated attack on cities throughout South Vietnam. Although they sustained heavy losses in the strike, known as the Tet Offensive, the bold move showed the United States that their enemy was much stronger than thought. Furthermore, because the attack came as a surprise, it rattled the American public's faith in the Johnson administration's prosecution of the war. A second significant event was the defense of Khe Sanh, a remote American military base. When the United States learned that the NVA was planning to lay siege to the military base, it decided to try to hold the base. Although the NVA abandoned the siege after seventy-seven days, the American troops stationed there had suffered heavy losses. Furthermore, when the NVA moved on, the United States abandoned the base, causing many to wonder why its defense had been important in the first place. Finally, the brutality of the war came home to many Americans when they learned of the massacre at the village of My Lai, when American soldiers rounded up and killed hundreds of unarmed Vietnamese civilians. Although many Americans could understand that the soldiers had been driven to the brink of madness by the harsh conditions of war, the incident made many doubt that the war was the noble enterprise its promoters had promised.

The documents in this chapter explore the war as it was experienced by those who fought it and offer perspectives on several of its defining moments.

The Vietcong: A Mortal Enemy

U.S. Department of Defense

The Vietnam War pitted the United States and the Republic of South Vietnam against Communist North Vietnam and against the Vietcong, the militant arm of the National Liberation Front, a revolutionary group within South Vietnam. Although not all members of the National Liberation Front were Communists, the name Vietcong, or "Vietnamese Communist," was used by the United States and its allies to refer to this largely underground military movement. The following U.S. Department of Defense publication, issued to armed forces personnel in 1966, was designed to educate the American soldier about the nature of the Vietcong.

As you read, consider the following questions:
1. According to the Department of Defense, how did the Vietcong traditionally win the support of the citizens of South Vietnam?
2. What kinds of tactics does the Department of Defense say the Vietcong uses to develop discipline within the ranks?
3. What do you think the difficulties would be fighting an enemy that uses what the Department of Defense calls the "Four Fast, One Slow" tactical doctrine?

Literally translated, the phrase Viet Cong (VC) means Vietnamese Communist, and those who are Viet Cong employ the whole Communist arsenal of deceit and violence. A Viet Cong is a man, woman, or child—a tough fighter, with

U.S. Department of Defense, *Know Your Enemy: The Viet Cong*. Washington, DC: Armed Forces Information and Education, 1966.

words or weapons, for what he is taught to call the "liberation" of South Vietnam—the Republic of Vietnam. Viet Cong also applies to the military and civilian components of the "Front" (the National Front for the Liberation of South Vietnam, or NFLSVN). To its deluded followers the Front is the government they serve—but to the vast majority of South Vietnamese it is an instrument of terror and oppression manipulated by the Communists of North Vietnam.

The Viet Cong, the Communist "Liberation Army" within the Republic of Vietnam, has expanded its numbers enormously, despite increasingly heavy casualties. Its so-called main force has grown from about 10,000 men in 1960 to over 65,000. Several regiments of the North Vietnamese Army have been sent by Hanoi into South Vietnam as part of the Communist buildup of forces in the south. As befits "regulars," many are armed with late-model imported weapons and wear uniforms, helmets of wicker or steel, and even scarves for unit identification. From isolated companies their formations have grown to battalions and regiments.

The strength of the Viet Cong guerrillas has not increased as rapidly. The estimated more than 100,000 guerrillas and militia, mostly based in the vicinity of their home villages and hamlets, are essential to the success of the main force and to the whole Viet Cong effort. Better armed and trained than before, the irregulars still wear the "calico noir," the traditional black pajamas of the Vietnamese peasant (worn also by the regulars as fatigue uniforms). They guide, support, reinforce, and provide recruits for the "liberation" movement. They also make possible the rule of the Communist Party in the countryside, enforcing the dictates of the local puppet Front organizations.

There are substantial areas in which the Front is the only effective government. It operates schools and hospitals, clothing factories and arsenals. Millions of Vietnamese support the Front out of friendship or fear, most often the latter. Due largely to the militia and the secret agents of the Party, an estimated one-fourth of the people of South Vietnam pay taxes to the Front, even though they may also pay taxes to the legitimate Government. This is an impressive record for a shadow government.

The Rise of the Viet Cong

What makes the Viet Cong and their way of warfare so significant is that they started with so little in material assets, although they had a belief in a well-proven doctrine (of subversion), a thorough knowledge of its tactics, and the moral support of their fellow Communists throughout the world. They had no industrial capacity. They had no substantial armed forces, only a few thousand experienced guerrillas, and perhaps 100,000 supporters—mostly in remote areas seldom visited by Government representatives.

On the other hand, the Viet Cong had hidden stores of weapons and ammunition left over from the war against the French. They had many trained and dedicated Communists to provide leadership, and access to the resources of the Communist regime in the North. Finally, the Vietnamese Communists—North and South—were united in their determination to use whatever means were necessary to bring the whole country under Communist domination. Without massive U.S. and free world support, South Vietnam might already have been added to the list of lost countries. . . .

Winning Support from the People

Although few, except those immediately affected, realized the war was on in the late 1950's and early 1960's, those who were the victims of the savage campaigns of terrorism, assassination, and kidnapping in rural Vietnam were well aware of it. So too were the thousands of cadres—trained, dedicated, hard-core Communist leaders and military officers—who fanned out in the countryside to win support for the insurgent forces. A cadre's role can be described as a combination priest, policeman, and propagandist. He is the Party and the Front in the countryside hamlets and villages. How they operate is graphically described by one of them, Captain Lam.

"We seek to do three things. The first is to drive a wedge

between the people and their government—to make the people hate their government, and the Americans. Our second objective is to get people to join our (VC) armed forces. The third is to persuade them to increase their production of food, and give the increase to us.

"Our cadre go into each village to study the situation and the people. Once they know the people and their problems, our cadre can explain how these problems are the fault of the government, and how the people can achieve their ambitions by following us. In this way we make the people hate their government, and can destroy the government in their village. Then we guide them in forming their own government (under our control) and in organizing their own armed forces, which of course are our auxiliaries.

"Of course we cannot do this right away in those villages and districts where the government is strong. There we concentrate on educating people politically to hate their government, and on forming both open and secret organizations which can support us, or embarrass the government. Every little bit helps. Any voluntary action of the people, from organized protests to simply slowing down on work ordered by the government, is a clear gain for us.

"Our cadre live in the village, or, if this is not safe, very close by. They appeal to the ideals, the patriotism, and the emotions of each individual according to his situation, and try to recruit him for the cause. If a person is arrested by government forces we try to contact him as soon as he is released, sympathize with him, arouse his hatred of the government, and recruit him. Many times we bring hungry, tired troops into a village so that the people may see how we are suffering for them, and arouse their sympathy. We try in every possible way to create hatred for the government and the Americans, to separate the people from the government and to make them see that we are their only hope."

Today, with the increase in Viet Cong forces, more emphasis is placed on terror and murder ("destroying the village government") and less on persuasion. Organizing and involving everyone possible in a maximum effort, coupled with incessant propaganda, is still emphasized as essential to Viet Cong success. . . .

Viet Cong Discipline

Scholar or street urchin, professional officer or farm boy, they all tell the same story of relentless indoctrination—of discipline playing on every human emotion, constantly applied. The soldier is required to memorize basic codes of conduct (a 10-point oath of honor and a 12-point code of discipline) which put him in the position of a hero, a patriot, a friend, and protector of the people. He is never allowed to forget this role. Perhaps the most effective reminder is his unit's daily indoctrination and self-criticism session. In this, his indoctrination is continued and reinforced, his supposed motives are reviewed and discussed by the group, and he is told by his leader what his future actions will be. After this, he must explain his reactions, and he must publicly confess and criticize his own shortcomings and weaknesses in thought and deed.

After every fight there is an almost immediate critique, with no holds barred, which gives every man a chance to let off steam. It also lets the cadre know what his men are thinking. This contributes to the effectiveness of the constant surveillance program, maintained primarily through the cell system (usually three-man) which is applied to every possible unit.

Appeals to the mind and the heart are the principal way in which the Viet Cong seeks to control its members. Regular units employ standard forms of military courtesy, and strict obedience is always expected, but emphasis is placed on making compliance with regulations appear to be voluntary. For those who fail in their duty, if such normal punishments as public criticism, extra duty, and brief confinement do not bring reform, the penalty is often discharge, in terms that make the man feel a traitor and an outcast from the human race. The fear of corporal punishment or death seems to be of less importance although either may be visited on the individual or his relatives.

Attention to Planning

It has been said that the Viet Cong soldier probably is told the reason for everything that he does more frequently and in greater detail than any other soldier in the world. Almost certainly he is required to explain the reasons for his actions more than any other soldier. Every proposed action is discussed from all angles before it is taken—and by everyone concerned except the targets and the innocent bystanders. Concerning the bystanders, one Viet Cong commented on the bombing of the U.S. Embassy, "If a few people get killed from a blast it is a risk of the war. . . . The Front is the benefactor of all the people."

Captain Lam's description of what happens after action against an RVNAF [Republic of Vietnam Armed Forces] outpost is recommended shows the almost incredible effort to make sure that everyone "gets the word" and performs his assigned duties.

"After studying the proposal. I report it to the head of the Provincial Military Affairs Committee. He then studies it from all points of view, considering especially the political effects, and the relative capabilities of our forces and those of the RVNAF. If he approves of the proposed operation he presents it to the Secretary of the Provincial Committee of the Party. The Secretary studies it and if he thinks it sound he calls a meeting of the whole Party Committee to study, discuss, and perhaps approve the proposal.

"Once the proposal is approved by the Party Committee, the Military Affairs Committee divides the preliminary tasks among its three staffs. The Military Staff sends a reconnaissance unit to study the objective from a military point of view, and to prepare a sandtable mock-up. The Political Staff sends a cadre to contact the civilians in the area, to learn their reaction to the [proposed] attack. It also studies the morale of the troops to see if they are mentally and emotionally prepared. If they are not, the Political Staff must take the necessary measures to prepare them. The Rear Services [logistics] Staff finds out if the civilians can furnish the necessary food and labor, including that needed for removal of the dead and of any booty.

"When all this is done, the Military Affairs Committee holds another meeting. This will be attended by the leaders of all the units that will be involved in the attack. If the majority of the Committee believes that the attack should be made, they report to another meeting of the Provincial Party Committee, which again reviews the proposed problem and the solution and perhaps directs some additional action. The Party Committee will approve the attack only if all conditions—political, military, and logistic—appear favorable.

"After this is accomplished all units begin practicing for the attack, either on a sandtable or an actual stake-and-string replica of the target. This practice will take from five days to a month, depending on the difficulty of the target, until every man knows just what he is supposed to do, how he is supposed to do it, and when. Every detail of the action will be planned out, including when and where the main force units will meet the local force and militia units. The militia are always necessary to guide the troops and to provide laborers to carry supplies, to carry off the booty and our dead, if any. We always try to carry away all our dead, to give them proper burial, which will comfort their families and strengthen the morale of the rest."

Such detailed preparation seems fantastic, but account after account bears it out. *Any* planned operation, whether an attack, an ambush, or a raid on a hamlet, is planned and rehearsed in great detail—and then often called off at the last moment when some factor has changed.

Viet Cong tactical doctrine is explicit. It is summarized in four words: Four Fast, One Slow. This means Fast Advance, Fast Assault, Fast Clearance of the Battlefield, and Fast Withdrawal—all based on Slow Preparation.

Battlefield Strategy

There is little that is new or unusual in Viet Cong tactical doctrine, once the basic principle of careful, thorough preparation for any contingency, followed by swift action, is grasped. Attacks on strongpoints almost always feature maximum use of explosives on a primary and a secondary objective, usually mutually supporting, *and* a careful deployment of forces to intercept or ambush any reinforcements that may be brought in. In several recent battles there have been indications of deliberate efforts to entice and ambush helicopter-borne troops.

In the past the Viet Cong have usually sought to avoid defensive combat unless they had the battlefield so organized that it was essentially an ambush. Nevertheless they carefully prepare for defense, with alternate and switch positions, in case they do decide to make a stand. Frequently these positions are incorporated into existing dikes separating rice fields so that emplacements seem to be merely breaks in the walls, and even trenches look like canals. Where the water level will permit, especially in the so-called secret base areas, elaborate tunnels are often constructed, both for cover and for concealment from ground and air forces. Like the Japanese in World War II, the Viet Cong are tireless diggers.

Controlled land mines, buried in highways and detonated when a Government target is over them, have long been a favorite and an economical Viet Cong method of destroying or at least discouraging their opponents. Occasionally nonmilitary targets are mined, usually by mistake or for some specific political or psychological purpose, such as warning uncooperative civilians. Homemade booby traps, ranging from simple deadfalls and "spikeboards" to explosive foot-mines are often used in preparing for a battle or an ambush, being placed in the covered areas the ambushees would naturally seek.

Like the elaborate trench-works often seen, the hundreds of booby traps around "liberated," meaning Viet-Cong-controlled, villages have some value if a Viet Cong unit decides to fight there. Their most important function, really, is to implicate the civilians in anti-Government actions. Government forces are likely to treat them as Viet Cong. The villagers fully anticipate this, so they feel forced to support the Viet Cong as their only hope. Secondarily, the trenches and the dugouts do provide protection for the civilians if the community is bombed or shelled by Government forces. Even though these attacks are provoked by the Viet Cong, the people are often grateful to these same provocateurs for "helping us to protect ourselves."

The Viet Cong's emphasis on carefully planned, discussed, and rehearsed actions has its disadvantages. If such an action fails, if losses are heavier than expected or not in proportion to benefits achieved, there is a corresponding drop in morale and combat effectiveness. An unexpected serious attack by Republic of Vietnam forces, especially when the resistance is unsuccessful, indicates poor planning by Viet Cong leaders and seriously impairs effectiveness for weeks or months, longer than the actual damage inflicted would warrant. Only a quick, successful counteraction can overcome this effect.

Viet Cong "Persuasion"

Much is said about the Viet Cong use of terror, which seems to be increasing. This is natural as the pace of the war steps up and support requirements grow faster than voluntary contributions. Taxes have been raised repeatedly in some areas. "Draftees" must fill in as voluntary recruiting proves inadequate. Terror-punishment seems to produce the fastest results, but it eventually reacts against those who use it unless they succeed in seizing complete power. Today, in many areas, the Viet Cong are faced with the administrative problems that afflict any government in time of war—and are losing voluntary support as a result.

The Viet Cong have, from the beginning, made every effort to secure the support of members of the Republic of Vietnam Armed Forces as well as the support of the civilians. Generally similar tactics have been used, emphasizing always the benefits to the individual and the high moral and patriotic worth of such a shift in allegiance. "Serve your country against the American imperialists," they say. "Don't be fooled because the Americans are more clever than the French; the Americans' motives are the same, but they use you as puppets."

The general preference for the "soft-sell" does not keep the Communists from killing, often by torture, whole garrisons of small posts they overwhelm when it seems appropriate to punish determined resistance or to frighten others in the area. Not infrequently one or two leaders will be brutally murdered as an example to the others. The dependents of the men may meet the same fate. Threats of reprisals against families are sometimes used as well. . . .

Most significant, and most dangerous for both sides, the Viet Cong pretense of being truly a South Vietnam "people's army" is rapidly being destroyed by the introduction on a growing scale of North Vietnamese forces and equipment—and by their own stepped-up actions as well. If this effort to achieve a quick victory fails, as our increasing support of the free Vietnamese is intended to assure, they say they are quite prepared to continue for 10 or 20 years if necessary and possible.

The war in Vietnam "is a different kind of war," said President [Lyndon] Johnson on July 28, 1965. "There are no marching armies or solemn declarations. Some citizens of South Vietnam, at times with understandable grievances, have joined in the attack on their own Government. But we must not let this mask the central fact that this is really war. It is guided by North Vietnam and it is spurred by Communist China. Its goal is to conquer the South, to defeat American power and to extend the Asiatic dominion of communism."

The Viet Cong is a tough enemy, but no tougher than his opponents. He is not a superman, nor is he invincible.

The Tet Offensive May Decide the War

The Economist

January 31, 1968, was the first day of Tet Mau Than, the new lunar year in Vietnam. It was also the first day of a major coordinated Communist assault on the cities of South Vietnam that came to be known as the Tet Offensive. The following article, originally published in the *The Economist* magazine on February 3 of that year, argues that the Tet Offensive is the first—and long-awaited—big battle of the Vietnam War, and it predicts that the outcome of the war may well hinge on how well the Communist effort fares.

As you read, consider the following questions:
1. Why does the *The Economist* say the Tet Offensive may well have political, rather than military, objectives?
2. According to the *The Economist*, what factors may have influenced the timing of the Tet Offensive?
3. Why does the *The Economist* think the Tet Offensive may well be the decisive moment of the Vietnam War?

General [Vo Nguyen] Giap [of North Vietnam] has set it rolling. This is the big battle, at last. Beautifully synchronised, and timed for the middle of the truce, the action he opened this week [January 31, 1968] should settle the Vietnam war one way or the other. General Giap is one of the best tactical commanders of our generation. He seizes the local initiative by moving his troops faster than anyone has a right to expect given the other side's control of the air. And he is a master of the surprise diversion. This week's at-

The Economist, "This Is It," *The Economist*, vol. 226, February 3, 1968, pp. 9–10. Copyright © 1968 by The Economist Newspaper Ltd. Reproduced by permission. Further reproduction prohibited. www.economist.com.

tacks by the Vietcong on eleven South Vietnamese cities un-mistakably bear his stamp: though the Vietcong is nomi-nally an independent army, its last known commander was a North Vietnamese general and it does not plunge in like this unless General Giap gives the word. In all these things—and in the way he cannot stop himself jumping in to take tactical control at the key moment in the fight—General Giap is remarkably like another great tactical com-mander: Erwin Rommel [World War II Nazi commander].

But he may resemble Rommel in another way too. Rom-mel in north-west Europe in 1944 was a master-tactician trying to cope with what he knew was in the long run a strategically hopeless situation. The more one looks at the offensive General Giap has been running since the autumn, and which led to the attacks on the towns this week, the more it looks as if its real aim is not a military one at all. Its aim is political: if possible, to shake American public opin-ion into electing a peace-making president in November; failing that, to get negotiations going on relatively favourable terms before the Americans' firepower eats deeper and deeper into the communists' hold of the back-country. General Giap might have preferred to hold his hand until closer to November, but he is obliged to strike now because the weather will turn against him in the spring. It is an attempt, conducted with brilliant tactical dash, to force a settlement before it is too late.

Battle Prospects
Three years ago, before the Americans sent their army in, these attacks on South Vietnam's cities would have been the last stage of the guerillas' war: having mastered the countryside, they would have been mopping up the towns according to [Chinese Communist chairman] Mao's sched-ule. Unless everybody has been wrong about Vietnam, they are not capable of this now. The Americans have been made to look foolish by losing control of part of their own embassy in Saigon. They will be in serious trouble if they and their allies cannot root the Vietcong squads out of all

the cities attacked this week. But it is very difficult for little bands of men with small arms to hold out in street-fighting against a determined regular army. The last people who tried holding a city against armoured troops were the Hungarians in 1956, and remember what happened to them. And if the allies do regain control, this week's attacks will look in retrospect liked pretty desperate adventure. The casualty count—it was 5,000 Vietcong against 530 allied dead by Thursday, though the figures may conceal a lot of civilian casualties—was bound to go against the attackers: that is what happens when you throw yourselves at the enemy's strongpoints. The probability is that it will also end up as a propaganda defeat for the Vietcong. Certainly the Vietcong could not be stopped from getting into the cities. That will impress the nervous. But in doing so the suicide squads have caused a lot of civilian deaths. This time it is the Vietcong's victims in the horror-pictures: that should help to restore the balance of emotion about this war.

For a time, at mid-week, a lot of people thought that this was the big attack and that the communist build-up around Khe Sanh [an American base] in the north-west corner of the country was a diversion to pull American troops away. It is almost certainly the other way round. It is at Khe Sanh that General Giap is looking for a victory that will achieve his political purpose; the raids on the cities are a diversion to draw the Americans' attention away from the testing place.

The Effect of Bombing

The campaign that General Giap launched at the end of last summer has followed a perfectly clear pattern. First he made an artillery attack on the marines' base at Con Thien, near the demilitarised zone in the far north. The Americans duly sent reinforcements scurrying up from farther south. He then launched his North Vietnamese and Vietcong infantry, from jumping-off points in Cambodia and Laos, into a series of attacks starting in the south and moving steadily northwards: at Loc Ninh, Dak To and now Khe Sanh. The fact that each new attack has taken place to the north of the previous one is a tribute to the effect of the Americans' bombing of his supply lines. It takes him about eight weeks, under this hammering from the air, to assemble a force big enough for a major fight. If President [Lyndon] Johnson had called off the bombing, General Giap could have put in more attacks, at quicker intervals, and he could have darted from point to point much more nimbly. At Khe Sanh he is now at the stump-end of his supply lines. The battle that is presumably going to take place at Khe Sanh this month may be his last chance of taking the offen-

This picture was taken in Saigon in 1968 during the Tet Offensive, the first big battle of the Vietnam War.

sive before the monsoon clears away from this part of Vietnam in April; and when the monsoon goes the sky will be wide open to the Americans' airpower.

This was the setting for this week's attacks on the cities. The decision to set the whole campaign under way was presumably taken in the middle of last summer, when the American public opinion polls began to show a sharp decline in the Americans' popular support for the war. The communist attacks at Loc Ninh and Dak To were bloody failures, and in December the polls seemed to show that the Americans were recovering their self-confidence. It is all the more important for North Vietnam that the Khe Sanh attack should succeed. This must be why President Ho Chi Minh took the enormous risk of giving the Vietcong the order to go for the cities. It is something he never dared to do before, even in the chaotic months of 1965 and early 1966 when the Saigon government was rocking on its feet and the Americans had just started coming ashore to help it out. If he is taking the risk now, it is because he feels he must.

The confrontation now taking place could well be decisive. President Ho and General Giap know the score. So far this winter they have lost the big-unit battles. The communists have taken far heavier casualties than the Americans have; American opinion at home has hardened in support of the war. Nor has the decision to draw the Americans into a series of big battles stopped the allies from slowly whittling down the area the Vietcong controls. The statistics are moving against the communists where it matters: in the number of people under each side's governance; in the miles of roads relatively secure from attack; in the casualty ratios. They are moving slowly, but they are moving. And North Vietnam's leaders know that after the presidential election there will be very little they can do to recapture the advantage.

Urgent Timing

The next President, if he is still committed to the war, will have three years in which he can ram the allies' military superiority home virtually at will. The Russians and the Chinese have made their position pretty plain. One or both of them might intervene if North Vietnam were invaded, though even that is far from certain. But short of that they are leaving it to the North Vietnamese. If the Vietnamese communists accept the failure of their attempt to put their sort of government into power in Saigon, Russia and China will accept it too.

So unless General Giap's regulars and the Vietcong irregulars do something about it now, they will be on a long, unstoppable slide downhill. And "now" means by April, when the planes will once more have an uninterrupted view through the clouds in the northern part of the country, which is the part General Giap can still get at. It has always been obvious that this war will have to end in a political settlement. Neither side wants, or has the power, to kill or capture the entire enemy army. The question is whether it will be a settlement that makes South Vietnam into a communist-run country or leaves it to develop under a pluralist system. It is a decision that will send its effects rippling through the rest of southern Asia. The big push that has now begun—General Giap's right hook at the Khe Sanh, coupled with the Vietcong's demonstration in the towns—is intended to hustle Mr Johnson into accepting the sort of negotiations that will eventually leave South Vietnam to the communists; or, if Mr Johnson won't, to frighten the Americans into electing someone else who will. It is up to the soldiers. If the allies cannot reassert their control over Saigon and the other big towns, the Americans will have to negotiate their way on to the troopships. But if they hold the towns, and stop Giap at Khe Sanh, they will have won the upper hand in the war, and in the peace talks.

The Closure of Khe Sanh Is Tactically Sound

W.W. Rostow

In January 1968 American military commanders and President Lyndon Johnson became aware of the fact that the North Vietnamese army was planning a siege of Khe Sanh, a remote American military base in the northernmost part of South Vietnam. The Americans decided to try to hold the base, and the five thousand soldiers stationed there hunkered down to wait out the siege, which lasted seventy-seven days. The outpost was surrounded by between twenty thousand and twenty-five thousand Communist troops, and the U.S. command feared that Khe Sanh would become the American Dien Bien Phu—the site of a decisive French defeat, by siege, in 1954. When Communists eventually relocated the bulk of the forces they had committed to Khe Sanh, the United States abandoned the base, causing many critics to charge that the base had been a meaningless objective the whole time. To those who pursued this line of reasoning, the American military strategy in Vietnam, of which Khe Sanh was an example, was often ill suited to countering a largely guerrilla army for whom the achievement of territorial goals was not an important objective. In the following draft of a proposed announcement explaining why the United States had abandoned Khe Sanh, Special Assistant for National Security Affairs W.W. Rostow offers a different interpretation of the move. He describes the battle at Khe Sanh as a success and the closure of the base as a sound tactical maneuver.

W.W. Rostow, "Draft of Proposed Announcement to be Made by MACV," http://members.easyspace.com/airdrop, June 25, 1968.

As you read, consider the following questions:

1. What goals were achieved by the U.S. military at Khe Sanh, according to the memorandum?
2. What are the two significant changes in the situation that warrant a shift in American tactics, according to Rostow?
3. What will the new American plan of action be, according to the memorandum?

---

1. The enemy was engaged at Khe Sanh earlier this year in order to combat him in the hinterlands rather than in the populated areas, to take maximum advantage of our air power and artillery, to prevent him from making a logistical base on the Quang Tri plateau and to sit astride the various potential infiltration routes.

2. General [William C.] Westmoreland achieved all of these goals. He kept two enemy divisions tied down, destroyed more than half of the 20 to 25,000 troops which the enemy had committed, prevented the establishment of the logistical base and helped block the potential infiltration routes.

3. We now intend to reinforce the successess won by General Westmoreland at Khe Sanh.

4. There have been two significant changes in the situation since early this year. One is an increase in friendly strength, mobility and fire power, so that we are now more capable than we were of conducting both a mobile offense and defense in western Quang Tri. The second is the shift in Communist strength and tactics, necessitated because their earlier tactics resulted in disaster at Khe Sanh.

5. They are now confronting us throughout Vietnam with stand-off mortar and artillery attacks and with small ground attacks, attempting to evade our efforts to fix and destroy their large formations. Additionally, they have increased significantly their strength immediately south of the DMZ [demilitarized zone between North and South Vietnam]—from the equivalent of six divisions in I Corps in

January to the equivalent of at least eight divisions today.

6. Because of the increase in our strength, mobility and firepower, and of the change in Communist strength and tactics, we are now in a position to alter our own tactics.

7. During the battle of Khe Sanh, we took maximum advantage of our superior firepower. We now plan to take maximum advantage of our firepower plus our second great asset—our mobility. The concept of our new disposition will be not linear, but mobile. The initiative in western Quang Tri province has been ours since Operation Pegasus [the operation that cleared the land supply route to Khe Sanh]. We are now taking steps to assure that it will continue to be ours.

8. We will use mobile forces, tied to no specific terrain, to attack, intercept, reinforce or take whatever action is most appropriate.

9. To take maximum advantage of the change in the enemy posture, we will close down the base at Khe Sanh. Having suffered one debacle with his earlier tactics at Khe Sanh, it is not logical to assume that the North Vietnamese would repeat that debacle. And it is not logical for us to be inflexible under the changed conditions.

10. I obviously am not going to go into details of precisely how we are deploying our forces or how we will utilize the additional maneuverability that we will gain by inactivating the base.

The My Lai Massacre

Ron Ridenhour

In the spring of 1969 a letter written by Ron Ridenhour, a
Vietnam veteran, reached various congressmen and public
officials in the United States. The letter reported something
remarkable: that Ridenhour had heard from numerous fellow servicemen that on March 16, 1968, American soldiers
had cold-bloodedly slaughtered nearly all the inhabitants of
the village of My Lai. In his letter, reprinted below, Ridenhour appeals to the U.S. Congress to investigate these allegations. Although the military began an investigation and
charged William Calley with murder in September 1969,
word of the massacre did not reach the American public until the journalist Seymour Hersh published an account of his
discussions with Ridenhour. The gruesome story seriously
undermined public confidence in the military, underscored
the brutality and inhumanity of war, and raised questions
about the quality of leadership training within the armed
forces. Ultimately, Calley alone was convicted and sen-
tenced to life in prison, but he was released in 1974.

As you read, consider the following questions:
1. What was Ridenhour's initial reaction to hearing about
   the massacre at My Lai?
2. Why did Ridenhour write his letter to members of the
   U.S. Congress?

It was late in April, 1968 that I first heard of "Pinkville"
and what allegedly happened there. I received that first report with some skepticism, but in the following months I
was to hear similar stories from such a wide variety of

Ron Ridenhour, "Letter to US Congress, March 29, 1969," www.fertel.com,
March 29, 1969.

people that it became impossible for me to disbelieve that something rather dark and bloody did indeed occur sometime in March, 1968 in a village called "Pinkville" in the Republic of Viet Nam.

The circumstances that led to my having access to the reports I'm about to relate need explanation. I was inducted in March, 1967 into the U.S. Army. After receiving various training I was assigned to the 70th Infantry Detachment (LRP), 11th Light Infantry Brigade at Schofield Barracks, Hawaii, in early October, 1967. That unit, the 70th Infantry Detachment (LRP), was disbanded a week before the 11th Brigade shipped out for Viet Nam on the 5th of December, 1967. All of the men from whom I later heard reports of the "Pinkville" incident were reassigned to "C" Company, 1st Battalion, 20th Infantry, 11th Light Infantry Brigade. I was reassigned to the aviation section of Headquarters Company 11th LIB. After we had been in Viet Nam for 3 to 4 months many of the men from the 70th Inf. Det. (LRP) began to transfer into the same unit, "E" Company, 51st Infantry (LRP).

In late April, 1968 I was awaiting orders for a transfer from HHC, 11th Brigade to Company "E," 51st Inf. (LRP), when I happened to run into Pfc [Private First Class] "Butch" Gruver, whom I had known in Hawaii. Gruver told me he had been assigned to "C" Company 1st of the 20th until April 1st when he transferred to the unit that I was headed for. During the course of our conversation he told me the first of many reports I was to hear of "Pinkville."

"Charlie" Company 1/20 had been assigned to Task Force Barker in late February, 1968 to help conduct "search and destroy" operations on the Batangan Peninsula, Barker's area of operation. The task force was operating out of L.Z. Dottie, located five or six miles north of Quang Nhai city on Vietnamese National Highway 1. Gruver said that Charlie Company had sustained casualties, primarily from mines and booby traps, almost everyday from the first day they arrived on the peninsula. One village area was particularly troublesome and seemed to be infested with booby traps and enemy soldiers. It was located about six miles northeast of Quang Nhai city at approximate coordinates B.S. 728795. It was a notorious area and the men of Task Force Barker had a special name for it: they called it "Pinkville." One morning in the latter part of March, Task Force Barker moved out from its firebase headed for "Pinkville." Its mission: destroy the trouble spot and all of its inhabitants.

A State of Disbelief

When "Butch" told me this I didn't quite believe that what he was telling me was true, but he assured me that it was and went on to describe what had happened. The other two companies that made up the task force cordoned off the village so that "Charlie" Company could move through to destroy the structures and kill the inhabitants. Any villagers who ran from Charlie Company were stopped by the encircling companies. I asked "Butch" several times if all the people were killed. He said that he thought they were, men, women and children. He recalled seeing a small boy, about three or four years old, standing by the trail with a gunshot wound in one arm. The boy was clutching his wounded arm with his other hand, while blood trickled between his fingers. He was staring around himself in shock and disbelief at what he saw. "He just stood there with big eyes staring around like he didn't understand; he didn't believe what was happening. Then the captain's RTO (radio operator) put a burst of 16 (M-16 rifle) fire into him." It was so bad, Gruver said, that one of the men in his squad shot himself in the foot in order to be medivaced out of the area so that he would not have to participate in the slaughter. Although he had not seen it, Gruver had been told by people he considered trustworthy that one of the company's officers, 2nd Lieutenant Kally (this spelling may be incorrect [the correct spelling is Calley]) had rounded up several groups of villagers (each group consisting of a minimum of 20 persons of both sexes and all ages). According to the story, Kally then machine-gunned each group. Gruver estimated that the population of the village had been 300 to 400 people and that very few, if any, escaped.

After hearing this account I couldn't quite accept it. Somehow I just couldn't believe that not only had so many young American men participated in such an act of barbarism, but that their officers had ordered it. There were other men in the unit I was soon to be assigned to, "E" Company, 51st Infantry (LRP), who had been in Charlie Company at the time that Gruver alleged the incident at "Pinkville" had occurred. I became determined to ask them about "Pinkville" so that I might compare their accounts with Pfc Gruver's.

When I arrived at "Echo" Company, 51st Infantry (LRP) the first men I looked for were Pfcs Michael Terry and William Doherty. Both were veterans of "Charlie" Company, 1/20 and "Pinkville." Instead of contradicting "Butch" Gruver's story they corroborated it, adding some tasty tidbits of information of their own. Terry and Doherty had been in the same squad and their platoon was the third platoon of "C" Company to pass through the village. Most of the people they came to were already dead. Those that weren't were sought out and shot. The platoon left nothing alive, neither livestock nor people. Around noon the two soldiers' squad stopped to eat. "Billy and I started to get out our chow," Terry said, "but close to us was a bunch of Vietnamese in a heap, and some of them were moaning. Kally (2nd Lt. Kally) had been through before us and all of them had been shot, but many weren't dead. It was obvious that they weren't going to get any medical attention so Billy and I got up and went over to where they were. I guess we sort of finished them off." Terry went on to say that he and Doherty then returned to where their packs were and ate lunch. He estimated the size of the village to be 200 to 300 people. Doherty thought that the population of "Pinkville" had been 400 people.

If Terry, Doherty and Gruver could be believed, then not only had "Charlie" Company received orders to slaughter all the inhabitants of the village, but those orders had come from the commanding officer of Task Force Barker, or possibly even higher in the chain of command. Pfc Terry stated that when Captain Medina (Charlie Company's commanding officer Captain Ernest Medina) issued the order for the destruction of "Pinkville" he had been hesitant, as if it were something he didn't want to do but had to. Others I spoke to concurred with Terry on this.

Mass Murder

It was June before I spoke to anyone who had something of significance to add to what I had already been told of the "Pinkville" incident. It was the end of June, 1968 when I ran into Sergeant Larry La Croix at the USO in Chu Lai. La Croix had been in 2nd Lt. Kally's platoon on the day Task Force Barker swept through "Pinkville." What he told me verified the stories of the others, but he also had something new to add. He had been a witness to Kally's gunning down of at least three separate groups of villagers. "It was terrible. They were slaughtering the villagers like so many sheep." Kally's men were dragging people out of bunkers and hootches and putting them together in a group. The people in the group were men, women and children of all ages. As soon as he felt that the group was big enough, Kally ordered an M-60 (machine-gun) set up and the people killed. La Croix said that he bore witness to this procedure at least three times. The three groups were of different sizes, one of about twenty people, one of about thirty people, and one of about forty people. When the first group was put together Kally ordered Pfc Torres to man the machine-gun and open fire on the villagers that had been grouped together. This Torres did, but before everyone in the group was down he ceased fire and refused to fire again. After ordering Torres to recommence firing several times, Lieutenant Kally took over the M-60 and finished shooting the remaining villagers in that first group himself. Sergeant La Croix told me that Kally didn't bother to order anyone to take the machine-gun when the other two groups of villagers were formed. He simply manned it himself and shot down all villagers in both groups.

This account of Sergeant La Croix's confirmed the rumors that Gruver, Terry and Doherty had previously told me about Lieutenant Kally. It also convinced me that there was a very substantial amount of truth to the stories that all of these men had told. If I needed more convincing, I was to receive it.

It was in the middle of November, 1968 just a few weeks before I was to return to the United States for separation from the army that I talked to Pfc Michael Bernhardt. Bernhardt had served his entire year in Viet Nam in "Charlie" Company 1/20 and he too was about to go home. "Bernie" substantiated the tales told by the other men I had talked to in vivid, bloody detail and added this. "Bernie" had absolutely refused to take part in the massacre of the villagers of "Pinkville" that morning and he thought that it was rather strange that the officers of the company had not made an issue of it. But that evening Medina (Captain Ernest Medina) came up to me ("Bernie") and told me "not to do anything stupid like write my congressman" about what had happened that day. Bernhardt assured Captain Medina that he had no such thing in mind. He had nine months left in Viet Nam and felt that it was dangerous enough just fighting the acknowledged enemy.

A Need for Action

Exactly what did, in fact, occur in the village of "Pinkville" in March, 1968 I do not know for *certain*, but I am convinced that it was something very black indeed. I remain irrevocably persuaded that if you and I do truly believe in the principles of justice and the equality of every man, however humble, before the law, that form the very backbone that this country is founded on, then we must press forward a widespread and public investigation of this matter with all our combined efforts. I think that it was Winston Churchill who once said "A country without a conscience is a country without a soul, and a country without a soul is a country that cannot survive." I feel that I must take some positive action on this matter. I hope that you will launch an investigation immediately and keep me informed of your progress. If you cannot, then I don't know what other course of action to take.

I have considered sending this to newspapers, magazines, and broadcasting companies, but I somehow feel that investigation and action by the Congress of the United States is the appropriate procedure, and as a conscientious citizen I have no desire to further besmirch the image of the American serviceman in the eyes of the world. I feel that this action, while probably it would promote attention, would not bring about the constructive actions that the direct actions of the Congress of the United States would.

The War from Inside

Mike Mancuso

For the American soldiers serving in the unfamiliar jungles of Vietnam, the postal service was their most important contact with "the World," as they called the mainstream American society from which they often felt far removed. The following letter was written in August 1970 from Private Mike Mancuso to his friend Mike Cook, a sergeant from Mancuso's brigade who was wounded in June 1970 by a booby trap. Mancuso asks about his friend's injury and reports on what has happened with the brigade since Cook was taken away with injuries. Both Mancuso and Cook survived the war and returned to the United States.

As you read, consider the following questions:
1. What tone does the letter adopt when Mancuso is talking about the injuries and deaths the brigade has suffered?
2. What effect do you think is created by Mancuso's use of slang that is specific to the Vietnam War?

I've been trying to write you for about a month it seems and for one reason or another never got down to it. You know how it is being in the field—you can't plan a damn thing.

So how are you doing? I really hope you'll be OK. You didn't look too good the last time I saw you, laying on that trail covered with blood. I really couldn't believe that damn thing went off. I heard the explosion and I hit the ground. There was shrapnel dropping all around me. I got up and saw Newcome about 10 to 12 meters farther down the trail rolling around. I went down there and he was bleeding.

Mike Mancuso, "Letter to Sgt. Michael Cook, August 26, 1970," *Dear America: Letters Home from Vietnam*, edited by Bernard Edelman. New York: W.W. Norton and Company, 1985. Copyright © 1985 by The New York Vietnam Veterans Memorial Commission. Reproduced by permission of Bernard Edelman.

And I thought, where the hell is Cook? There was still dust and dirt flying around so I couldn't see you.

So I called for the medic (good old Kiminski). He came down there and saw me putting a dressing on Newcome and said, "How is he?" I said "He's got titi [slang for "small" or "little"]. Take care of Cook." So he went to you. When I finished with Newcome I went to see how you were. I had no idea you were hit that bad. Then the dust-off came and I put all your gear on the bird [helicopter]. I was going to keep Newcome's 79 [an M-79 grenade launcher], but it was all bent to hell from the shrapnel. (If it hadn't hit the 79, it would be in his stomach. Lucky, huh?)

Then you were gone. I was messed up for two days, and I'm not even kiddin'. All I could think, what if you were dying or were dead when I was screwing around with New-come's shoulder? I really felt bad about that. No one to talk to, make fabulous C-rat [combat-rations] meals with, or pull guard with.

Newcome came back to the field the 23rd of August so he's A-OK. Can you believe our squad was down to two men? Suarez and myself. We were in bad shape.

The rest of that mission wasn't bad. Except for one day we were pinned down while humping [carrying packs and marching] out of a ville. They held us for about 30 minutes. We couldn't move. Salas was stuck in the middle of the trail and couldn't get up until Lester, Dadisman, Norton, Melisi, Griffin and myself put one burst of fire into that woodline that would have made King Kong get his head down. No one was hurt, and I can't see how we made it. [Smitty] called in "arty" [artillery] right on top of us. Lucky it was only a marker round, and even that was about 75 to 100 meters away. Good old [Smitty]. Still screw'n up by the numbers.

We moved into Dragon Valley and really hit some shit. Seven dinks [Vietcong] with 47s opened up on our day fog-ger. The first burst hit Dadisman—five rounds in the chest. Melisi hit by two ricochets only titi. Barker titi in the leg. Eller titi in the fingers. Duford shot through the hand. Jerry

Sholl got it in the hip—fractured it. They were all in one big cluster playing cards. They drew the fire. [Newman] shot himself with a short 79 round. It was really hell. It rained AK rounds like no one could imagine. Battels got hit. They couldn't even see him—they just shot up his hooch.

U.S. Marines search for North Vietnamese army bunkers

Battels is back in the World [the United States]. We don't know how he's doing. He was pretty bad—shot right through the lung. Jerry and Duford are back in the World, too. Dadisman, God rest his soul, is dead. We really took it bad. Especially Eller. Dadisman was sitting right next to him when it happened.

The day before this happened the 1st Platoon walked into a booby trap of claymores and hand frags [grenades] hooked up to a trip wire that was attached to a branch hanging in the middle of the trail. Someone hit it, and it went off. A new E-5 [military rank] and two new soul brothers [black soldiers] were killed. The lieutenant got it in the head. He's a vegetable now. Can't even talk. Moose got it almost in his eye. He's permanent OP [Out Post, or sentry duty] now.

Charlie Company had 22 men dusted off in two days. We were operating with 41 men in the field. We came on the hill and got 27 replacements out there in Happy Valley [An Lao Valley], now. And haven't seen or hit anything. Unusual, isn't it?

I'm sham'in now. I've been having a lot of trouble with my left arm. My ruck sack keeps pinching the nerves in my shoulder (remember when that started happening?), so I got a 30-day with no ruck sack and I have to go back to Da Nang hospital for a recheck. I was in the hospital for four days. I'm hoping for a permanent profile for not being able to carry a ruck sack.

I think you got out just at the right time. Consider yourself lucky you're not Dadisman or one of the other three who didn't make it. I'm keeping my fingers crossed for this profile.

I tried to cover the most important things that have happened since you left. I hope you can read and understand this letter without too much trouble. I can't possibly write all the details—it would take forever. I'm not trying to get you depressed by telling you about Dadisman and the rest of the men, but knowing you I thought you would be wondering what's happened here.

It's not very pretty, is it. It's happened before, happened then, and it will happen again. I just keep my fingers crossed. Stay out of clusters [groups of soldiers], and keep my distance while humping.

So be cool. Stay A-Head and Keep Peace.

Oh, yeah, there was one thing I wanted to tell you. Do you remember when we were out in the field and I couldn't get any "D" rings for my ruck sack? And you told me if someone goes in on a dust-off to take them off their ruck? *Well I did, thanks. They were on your ruck!* I laughed like hell when I thought about it later.

Write back and let me know how you are and what you're doing.

4

THE ANTIWAR MOVEMENT

CHAPTER PREFACE

For the U.S. government, the Vietnam War was fought on two fronts. Foremost, of course, was the battleground in Southeast Asia, where hundreds of thousands of Americans served and over fifty-eight thousand suffered fatal injuries. But there was another front, on American soil, where the government faced strong opposition from Americans opposed to the war.

There had always been people who protested American involvement in wars. The Quakers, for instance, had a long history of conscientious objection and had secured key court judgments that respected their religious prohibition against harming others. But the protests against the Vietnam War were different. Of course, some of those who protested were absolute pacifists who believed that war is always wrong. More often, however, those opposed to the war were not opposed to war in general but believed instead that this particular war was wrong. Furthermore, although the main thrust of the antiwar movement involved students and other young people, Americans from many different parts of society and of all age groups were involved in opposing the war.

The first large antiwar protests were held in the spring of 1966 in Washington, New York, Chicago, Boston, San Francisco, and Philadelphia. A year later, in the spring of 1967, there were huge demonstrations in New York and San Francisco against the war, and the respected civil rights leader Martin Luther King Jr. added his voice to those opposed to the war. One of the most dramatic protests took place in 1968 at the Democratic National Convention, where 26,000 police and national guardsmen met 10,000 antiwar protesters. In clashes with police, 800 protesters were injured. The rallies continued in 1969, even though President Richard Nixon had begun to slowly withdraw

American troops from Vietnam. In November of that year, a crowd of 250,000 gathered in Washington to oppose the war. The following spring, after Nixon announced that the United States had secretly extended the war into Cambodia, a neutral country, campuses across America erupted in protest. The number and intensity of the rallies only increased after National Guardsmen, in apparent confusion, opened fire and killed four students at Kent State University in Ohio on May 4, 1970. Similar protests continued until the end of the war, with 12,000 protesters being arrested at one dramatic rally in Washington in May 1971.

Those who opposed the war did so for various reasons. Some believed that America had no business fighting in a small overseas country that posed no threat to the United States. Some of these advocated a traditional isolationist approach to foreign affairs. Others believed that the war was one of imperialist aggression, in which the United States was interfering with the natural, democratic development of a sovereign nation. For many, what mattered was the fact that young American men were being drafted, and in many cases injured or killed, and that the mounting costs of the war diverted money from domestic social programs. Antiwar sentiment grew as American involvement deepened and as casualties mounted. At one point, even the widely respected news anchor Walter Cronkite editorialized on national television that the Vietnam War was a war the United States could not win. And some returning veterans spoke out against the war, which helped demonstrate that the movement consisted of more than hippies and draft dodgers.

The effects of the antiwar protests were hard to assess. Some critics charged that they aided the enemy by undermining the morale of American troops, but others insisted that the bulk of the protesters were misguided youth who had little understanding of international politics. The documents in this chapter explore the antiwar movement, offering perspectives both from those opposed to the war and from those who had serious criticisms of the movement.

A Call to Resist an Imperial and Savage War

May 2nd Movement

The following article, originally issued in September 1965, is a manifesto of the May 2nd Movement, an organization of U.S. students that draws its name from May 2, 1964, the date of the first significant student protests against U.S. involvement in Vietnam. The group harshly condemns American business activity abroad, which it sees as a kind of oppressive economic colonialism, and argues that the American military and educational system play a major role in supporting this system. In addition, the group calls on Americans, especially students, to actively resist the war.

As you read, consider the following questions:
1. What picture of the North Vietnamese Vietminh, against whom the United States was fighting, does the manifesto offer?
2. What are the problems with the educational system in the United States, according to the authors of the manifesto?
3. What specific actions are students and others urged to perform in order to resist the war in Vietnam?

We, as students in the richest but most brutally confused country in the world, cannot understand that world and our part in it with the ahistorical education we receive in our universities. In order to make ourselves into effective social beings and in order to discover, sharpen, and use the power

May 2nd Movement, "What Is the May 2nd Movement?" http://lists.village. virginia.edu/sixties, May 2, 1965. Copyright © 1993 by The Sixties Project. Reproduced by permission of The Sixties Project.

of our knowledge, we should organize ourselves in the broadest possible way to combat that lack of education. For it is a lack, a vacuum, that leads to political degeneration and default. The May 2nd Movement was formed to fight against a politics of default, specifically by organizing student protest and revolt against our government's savage war on the people of Vietnam.

May 2, 1964, saw the first major student demonstrations against the war in Vietnam. In New York City, 1,000 students marched through Times Square to the United Nations to protest what was then called "U.S. intervention" on behalf of the legitimate government of South Vietnam. More than 700 students and young people marched through San Francisco. In Boston, Madison, Wisconsin, Seattle, there were simultaneous smaller demonstrations. A start, but nowhere near enough. Nowhere near enough because very few students even knew about the war, or if they did, knew what it means, or what they could do about it. Now thousands know the nature of the war in Vietnam and its corollary deceit in the press and in our universities, and its concomitant at home. The May 2nd Movement calls that war and the resulting lies about it at home the products of an imperialistic system.

The chief imperialistic power in the world today is the United States, which has a business empire that permeates the non-socialist world, extracting the superprofits made possible by monopoly control. U.S. economic strangulation of other countries causes horrible living conditions, including mass starvation, to prevail. The people who live in these countries have tried every "legal," non-violent recourse to break out of their misery, only to be violently suppressed or granted phony independence, without political freedom or economic improvement. They are driven to revolution as the only means of liberation from imperialistic domination. To keep them down the U.S. business empire requires the largest military empire in world history. Besides 3,600 bases abroad, the U.S. military empire includes the "native troops," the U.S. trained, equipped and paid armies of the puppet military dictators (Ky, Tschombe, Branco[1]). Ruling their countries for the benefit of foreign business, getting personal wealth and power as their out, these traitors serve to conceal the foreign nature of their country's oppression.

The May 2nd movement opposes this 1965 version of imperialism—the corporations that exact superprofits, the military machine that enforces the system by violence and the cultural establishment that maintains the system abroad and at home, by racism, ignorance, lies and suppression of the socially creative forces within man himself.

National liberation movements are emerging in country after country around the world. Some have already been victorious: Cuba, North Vietnam, Indonesia, China. Others are carrying on pitched armed struggle against imperialism or are building toward it: Dominican Republic, Venezuela, Panama, Puerto Rico, British Guyana, Colombia, Guatemala, Brazil, Congo, South Africa, Rhodesia, Angola, Mozambique, Iran, Vietnam, Laos, Thailand, Philippines. This is the many-fronted third world war. The May 2nd Movement, recognizing that there can be no peace without freedom, supports and joins the struggles for national liberation. We defect politically from the corruption of culture, mind and body that is the price the privileged must pay in our country for a share in the booty of exploitation.

Complacent Universities

The university offers no explanation of what's wrong, of what's happening in a world principally marked by revolution. Instead, it grooms us for places as technicians, managers and clerks within the giant corporations, or to be professional apologists for the status quo within the giant multiversities, or to fit some other cog-space that needs the special "sensitivity" that only the polish of factory education can bring. University courses on China put forward

1. Nguyen Cao Ky, president of South Vietnam, 1965–1967; Moise Tschombe, leader of the Democratic Republic of the Congo, 1964–1965; General Humberto Branco, president of Brazil, 1964–1967.

the same formula as the war comic books—a communist conspiracy resulting in a blue-ant hill. Usually there is no course at all on revolutionary Cuba, one of the major developments of our lifetime, only 90 miles away. Philosophy is not interested in how to understand (let alone change) the world, only in how to evade it. Literature is concerned with form alone. Students jump from major to major in search of relevancy, then, finding it nowhere, either quit or settle for banality. The university is doing its job, supplying the system with loyal, well-trained, intelligent servants—who are moral, cultural and social morons. . . .

Out of this understanding of imperialism as responsible for the poverty of our lives, and out of the void of inaction of the existing peace and left groups on the campuses, the May 2nd Movement was formed. M2M is campus based, attempting to organize students to fight the system and not dociley (or gripingly) accept it.

The major issue facing U.S. students at this time is the war against the people of Vietnam. This war is also against the interests of the students and almost the entire population of the United States. Nine billion dollars has already been cut from the ever-decreasing "peace" portion of the federal budget. The war has been used against steel workers, who were told that they were not permitted to strike because of the "national emergency." The administration will demand that black Americans stop protesting in an attempt to cover angry faces with a mask of "national unity."

Most people realize that the U.S. is not fighting for freedom and democracy in Vietnam, that the Vietnamese people want nothing more than the U.S. to get out. We say to those who are being forced to kill and die for the interests of imperialism—*don't go*. The May 2nd Movement is launching an anti-induction campaign on the campuses. This campaign will organize existing resistance to the draft, based on the refusal to fight against the people of Vietnam. Each campus and each community should say, "No one from this college (or community) should be drafted." Declarations and literature will be circulated, forums and meetings held, demonstrations organized and acts of disobedience engaged in. The theme will be, *"We Won't Go."*

Resisting the War

We are beginning a program of approaching workers at the factory gate to talk to them about the war in Vietnam and why it is against the interests of workers. This project comes out of the understanding that while students make up an important section of the population, industrial workers make, load and transport the goods, and are therefore the key for stopping the war in Vietnam—for stopping the whole system. While workers' militancy has become more apparent in recent years, we realize that organizing a radical workers' movement in this country is a long range goal, and one that essentially must be done by workers. All the more reason to begin projects now to involve workers in the peace movement and as allies of the student.

Some chapters of May 2 plan campaigns to donate blood and other medical aid to the National Liberation Front of South Vietnam, to concretely show our support for national liberation struggles. Receiving blood from U.S. college students will be a terrific morale boost to the Vietnamese people. Collecting pledges for blood on campus can also show where the administration stands, as collecting for civil rights did at [the University of California at] Berkeley.

Vietnam is not the only slap in the face administered to students by U.S. foreign policy. During the summers of 1963 and 1964, 150 U.S. students traveled to Cuba to see the meaning of a Revolution. They went in spite of a state department "ban" on travel to Cuba. Even worse, they came back and told students throughout the country, with their experience and with slides, that Cuba was building a just society. The organizers of the trips (including members of M2M) face between five and twenty years in jail. We are now organizing defense for them on campuses. We must fight for our right to travel anywhere and see for ourselves what is happening—we don't find out in our classes and newspapers. The ban on travel to Cuba (and China, North

Korea, North Vietnam, liberated parts of South Vietnam, Albania) is not an isolated Civil Liberties issue. It is part of the U.S. government's policy of suppressing people around the world. Fighting against the ban is part of our struggle for liberation. . . .

When the student protest movement refers to "the establishment," we are not kidding. That which we are out to change—be it a university or a government—is built on a tremendously powerful structure of material and organization. The money and resources available to it are immense. We will change nothing unless we organize ourselves, forge ourselves into a united and disciplined force and match the strength of the establishment in confrontations. We can do so because our strength is based on people, not cash. M2M is building an organization of students that recognizes, and works to satisfy, our needs as students and as men and women. These needs are inseparable from the worldwide struggle for liberation. One can choose to oppose this struggle, or to join it. To oppose it is to be a murderer. To join together and fight to change this murderous society is the only way for any of us to live with decency and dignity. We will succeed when large numbers of students have the insight, the dedication and the will to organize themselves, to join the struggle with their sections of the population, and to see it through.

A Veteran Calls for the War to End

John Kerry

In April 1971 one thousand Vietnam veterans marched in Washington to call for an end to the war. In an address before the Senate Committee on Foreign Relations, reprinted below, John Kerry, a twenty-seven-year-old veteran who spoke for the group, accuses the U.S. military of perpetrating great harm in Vietnam. Kerry earned a silver star, a bronze star, and three purple hearts in Vietnam and is currently serving his fourth term as a Massachusetts senator.

As you read, consider the following questions:
1. According to Kerry, how did most Vietnamese view the conflict?
2. What do you think Kerry means when he says "we rationalized destroying villages in order to save them"?
3. Kerry mentions two different ways in which he thinks the American prosecution of the war was racist. What are those two ways?

I would like to talk on behalf of all those veterans and say that several months ago in Detroit we had an investigation at which over 150 honorably discharged, and many very highly decorated, veterans testified to war crimes committed in Southeast Asia. These were not isolated incidents but crimes committed on a day-to-day basis with the full awareness of officers at all levels of command. It is impossible to describe to you exactly what did happen in Detroit—the emotions in the room and the feelings of the men

John Kerry, address before the Senate Committee on Foreign Relations, April 3, 1971.

who were reliving their experiences in Vietnam. They relived the absolute horror of what this country, in a sense, made them do.

They told stories that at times they had personally raped, cut off ears, cut off heads, taped wires from portable telephones to human genitals and turned up the power, cut off limbs, blown up bodies, randomly shot at civilians, razed villages in fashion reminiscent of Ghengis Khan, shot cattle and dogs for fun, poisoned food stocks, and generally ravaged the countryside of South Vietnam in addition to the normal ravage of war and the normal and very particular ravaging which is done by the applied bombing power of this country.

We call this investigation the Winter Soldier Investigation. The term Winter Soldier is a play on words of Thomas Paine's in 1776 when he spoke of the Sunshine Patriots and summertime soldiers who deserted at Valley Forge because the going was rough.

We who have come here to Washington have come here because we feel we have to be winter soldiers now. We could come back to this country, we could be quiet, we could hold our silence, we could not tell what went on in Vietnam, but we feel because of what threatens this country, not the reds [Communists], but the crimes which we are committing that threaten it, that we have to speak out. . . .

In our opinion and from our experience, there is nothing in South Vietnam which could happen that realistically threatens the United States of America. And to attempt to justify the loss of one American life in Vietnam, Cambodia or Laos by linking such loss to the preservation of freedom, which those misfits supposedly abuse, is to us the height of criminal hypocrisy, and it is that kind of hypocrisy which we feel has torn this country apart.

We found that not only was it a civil war, an effort by a people who had for years been seeking their liberation from any colonial influence whatsoever, but also we found that the Vietnamese whom we had enthusiastically molded after our own image were hard put to take up the fight against the threat we were supposedly saving them from.

We found most people didn't even know the difference between communism and democracy. They only wanted to work in rice paddies without helicopters strafing them and bombs with napalm burning their villages and tearing their country apart. They wanted everything to do with the war, particularly with this foreign presence of the United States of America, to leave them alone in peace, and they practiced the art of survival by siding with whichever military force was present at a particular time, be it Viet Cong, North Vietnamese or American.

An Inside Perspective

We found also that all too often American men were dying in those rice paddies for want of support from their allies. We saw first hand how monies from American taxes were used for a corrupt dictatorial regime. We saw that many people in this country had a one-sided idea of who was kept free by the flag, and blacks provided the highest percentage of casualties. We saw Vietnam ravaged equally by American bombs and search and destroy missions, as well as by Viet Cong terrorism—and yet we listened while this country tried to blame all of the havoc on the Viet Cong.

We rationalized destroying villages in order to save them. We saw America lose her sense of morality as she accepted very coolly a My Lai [the name of a village where more than one hundred villagers were massacred by American soldiers] and refused to give up the image of American soldiers who hand out chocolate bars and chewing gum.

We learned the meaning of free fire zones, shooting anything that moves, and we watched while America placed a cheapness on the lives of orientals.

We watched the United States falsification of body counts, in fact the glorification of body counts. We listened while month after month we were told the back of the enemy was about to break. We fought using weapons against "oriental human beings." We fought using weapons against those people which I do not believe this country would dream of using were we fighting in the European theater. We watched while men charged up hills because a general said that hill has to be taken, and after losing one platoon or two platoons they marched away to leave the hill for reoccupation by the North Vietnamese. We watched pride allow the most unimportant battles to be blown into extravaganzas, because we couldn't lose, and we couldn't retreat, and because it didn't matter how many American bodies were lost to prove that point, and so there were Hamburger Hills and Khe Sanhs and Hill 81s and Fire Base 6s [various sites of battles or American entrenchments in Vietnam] and so many others.

Now we are told that the men who fought there must watch quietly while American lives are lost so that we can exercise the incredible arrogance of Vietnamizing the Vietnamese.

Each day to facilitate the process by which the United

Many South Vietnamese were left homeless after their villages were destroyed by warfare.

States washes her hands of Vietnam someone has to give up his life so that the United States doesn't have to admit something that the entire world already knows, so that we can't say that we have made a mistake. Someone has to die so that President [Richard] Nixon won't be, and these are his words, "the first President to lose a war."

Dying for a Mistake

We are asking Americans to think about that because how do you ask a man to be the last man to die in Vietnam? How do you ask a man to be the last man to die for a mistake? . . . We are here in Washington to say that the problem of this war is not just a question of war and diplomacy. It is part and parcel of everything that we are trying as human beings to communicate to people in this country—the question of racism which is rampant in the military, and so many other questions such as the use of weapons; the hypocrisy in our taking umbrage at the Geneva Conventions and using that as justification for a continuation of this war when we are more guilty than any other body of violations of those Geneva Conventions; in the use of free fire zones, harassment interdiction fire, search and destroy missions, the bombings, the torture of prisoners, all accepted policy by many units in South Vietnam. That is what we are trying to say. It is part and parcel of everything.

An American Indian friend of mine who lives in the Indian Nation of Alcatraz put it to me very succinctly. He told me how as a boy on an Indian reservation he had watched television and he used to cheer the cowboys when they came in and shot the Indians, and then suddenly one day he stopped in Vietnam and he said, "my God, I am doing to these people the very same thing that was done to my people," and he stopped. And that is what we are trying to say, that we think this thing has to end.

We are here to ask, and we are here to ask vehemently, where are the leaders of our country? Where is the leadership? We're here to ask where are McNamara, Rostow,

Bundy, Gilpatrick, and so many others?[1] Where are they now that we, the men they sent off to war, have returned? These are the commanders who have deserted their troops. And there is no more serious crime in the laws of war. The Army says they never leave their wounded. The marines say they never even leave their dead. These men have left all the casualties and retreated behind a pious shield of public rectitude. They've left the real stuff of their reputations bleaching behind them in the sun in this country. . . .

We wish that a merciful God could wipe away our own memories of that service as easily as this administration has wiped away their memories of us. But all that they have done and all that they can do by this denial is to make more clear than ever our own determination to undertake one last mission—to search out and destroy the last vestige of this barbaric war, to pacify our own hearts, to conquer the hate and fear that have driven this country these last ten years and more. And more. And so when thirty years from now our brothers go down the street without a leg, without an arm, or a face, and small boys ask why, we will be able to say "Vietnam" and not mean a desert, not a filthy obscene memory, but mean instead where America finally turned and where soldiers like us helped it in the turning.

1. Robert McNamara was secretary of defense from 1961 to 1968; Eugene Rostow was undersecretary of state for political affairs under President Lyndon Johnson and a noted defender of U.S. involvement in Vietnam; McGeorge Bundy was national security adviser to presidents John F. Kennedy and Johnson; Roswell Gilpatrick was deputy secretary of defense under McNamara.

The Antiwar Movement Threatens American Democracy

Spiro Agnew

Spiro Agnew, the U.S. vice president under Richard Nixon from 1969 to 1973, was known as a strong critic of Vietnam War protesters. In a series of speeches during his tenure as vice president, Agnew argued that many of those who opposed the war were not conscientious citizens exercising their right to disagree with their government but rather misguided and dangerously self-righteous individuals. In the following speech, delivered to a Republican dinner in the fall of 1969, Agnew defends and expands on remarks he had made in a speech a week earlier criticizing some elements of the protest movement.

As you read, consider the following questions:
1. What does Agnew mean when he speaks of the difference between using and abusing liberty?
2. What personal criticisms does Agnew make about some individuals in the antiwar movement?
3. What does Agnew fear will happen if the United States remains what he calls "a convulsive society"?

A little over a week ago, I took a rather unusual step for a Vice President . . . I said something. Particularly, I said something that was predictably unpopular with the people who would like to run this country without the inconvenience of seeking public office. I said I did not like some of

Spiro Agnew, address before a Republican dinner, Harrisburg, Pennsylvania, October 30, 1969.

the things I saw happening in this country. I criticized those who encouraged government by street carnival and suggested it was time to stop the carousel.

It appears that by slaughtering a sacred cow I triggered a holy war. I have no regrets. I do not intend to repudiate my beliefs, recant my words, or run and hide.

What I said before, I will say again. It is time for the preponderant majority, the responsible citizens of this country, to assert *their* rights. It is time to stop dignifying the immature actions of an arrogant, reckless, inexperienced element within our society. The reason is compelling. It is simply that their tantrums are insidiously destroying the fabric of American democracy.

By accepting unbridled protest as a way of life, we have tacitly suggested that the great issues of our times are best decided by posturing and shouting matches in the streets. America today is drifting toward Plato's classic definition of a degenerating democracy . . . a democracy that permits the voice of the mob to dominate the affairs of government.

Last week I was lambasted for my lack of "mental and moral sensitivity." I say that any leader who does not perceive where persistent street struggles are going to lead this nation lacks mental acuity. And any leader who does not caution this nation on the danger of this direction lacks moral strength.

Now let me make it clear, I believe in Constitutional dissent. I believe in the people registering their views with their elected representatives, and I commend those people who care enough about their country to involve themselves in its great issues. I believe in legal dissent within the Constitutional limits of free speech, including peaceful assembly and the right of petition. But I do not believe that demonstrations, lawful or unlawful, merit my approval or even my silence where the purpose is fundamentally unsound. In the case of the Vietnam Moratorium, the objective announced by the leaders—immediate unilateral withdrawal of all our forces from Vietnam—was not only unsound but idiotic. The tragedy was that thousands who participated wanted only to show a fervent desire for peace, but were used—yes, used—by the political hustlers who ran the event.

It is worth remembering that our country's founding fathers wisely shaped a constitutional republic, not a pure democracy. The representative government they contemplated and skillfully constructed never intended that elected officials should decide crucial issues by counting the number of bodies cavorting in the streets. They recognized that freedom cannot endure dependent upon referendum every time part of the electorate desires it.

So great is the latitude of our liberty that only a subtle line divides use from abuse. I am convinced that our preoccupation with emotional demonstration, frequently crossing the line to civil disruption and even violence could inexorably lead us across that line forever.

Ironically, it is neither the greedy nor the malicious, but the self-righteous who are guilty of history's worst atrocities. Society understands greed and malice and erects barriers of law to defend itself from these vices. But evil cloaked in emotional causes is well disguised and often undiscovered before it is too late.

Intolerant Critics
We have just such a group of self-proclaimed saviours of the American soul at work today. Relentless in their criticism of intolerance in America, they themselves are intolerant of those who differ with their views. In the name of academic freedom, they destroy academic freedom. Denouncing violence, they seize and vandalize buildings of great universities. Fiercely expressing their respect for truth, they disavow the logic and discipline necessary to pursue truth.

They would have us believe that they alone know what is good for America; what is true and right and beautiful. They would have us believe that their reflective action is superior to our reflective action; that their revealed righteousness is more effective than our reason and experience.

Think about it. Small bands of students are allowed to shut down great universities. Small groups of dissidents are allowed to shout down political candidates. Small cadres of professional protesters are allowed to jeopardize the peace efforts of the President of the United States.

It is time to question the credentials of their leaders. And, if in questioning we disturb a few people, I say it is time for them to be disturbed. If, in challenging, we polarize the American people, I say it is time for a positive polarization.

It is time for a healthy in-depth examination of policies and a constructive realignment in this country. It is time to rip away the rhetoric and to divide on authentic lines. It is time to discard the fiction that in a country of 200 million people, everyone is qualified to quarterback the government.

For too long we have accepted superficial categorization—young versus old; white versus black; rich versus poor. Now it is time for an alignment based on principles and values shared by all citizens regardless of age, race, creed, or income. This, after all, is what America is all about.

America's pluralistic society was forged on the premise that what unites us in ideals is greater than what divides us as individuals. Our political and economic institutions were developed to enable men and ideas to compete in the marketplace on the assumption that the best would prevail. Everybody was deemed equal, and by the rules of the game they could become superior. The rules were clear and fair: in politics, win an election; in economics, build a better mousetrap. And as time progressed, we added more referees to assure equal opportunities and provided special advantages for those whom we felt had entered life's arena at a disadvantage.

The majority of Americans respect these rules . . . and with good reason. Historically, they have served as a bulwark to prevent totalitarianism, tyranny, and privilege . . . the old world spectres which drove generations of immigrants to American sanctuary. Pragmatically, the rules of America work. This nation and its citizens—collectively and individually—have made more social, political and economic progress than any civilization in world history.

The principles of the American system did not spring up overnight. They represent centuries of bitter struggle. Our laws and institutions are not even purely American—only our federal system bears our unique imprimatur.

We owe our values to the Judeo-Christian ethic which stresses individualism, human dignity, and a higher purpose than hedonism. We owe our laws to the political evolution of government by consent of the governed. Our nation's philosophical heritage is as diverse as its cultural background. We are a melting pot nation that has for over two centuries distilled something new and, I believe, sacred.

Rotten Apples

Now, we have among us a glib, activist element who would tell us our values are lies, and I call them impudent. Because anyone who impugns a legacy of liberty and dignity that reaches back to Moses, is impudent.

I call them snobs for most of them disdain to mingle with the masses who work for a living. They mock the common man's pride in his work, his family and his country. It has also been said that I called them intellectuals. I did not. I said that they characterized themselves as intellectuals. No true intellectual, no truly knowledgeable person, would so despise democratic institutions.

America cannot afford to write off a whole generation for the decadent thinking of a few. America cannot afford to divide over their demagoguery . . . or to be deceived by their duplicity . . . or to let their license destroy liberty. We can, however, afford to separate them from our society—with no more regret than we should feel over discarding rotten apples from a barrel.

The leaders of this country have a moral as well as a political obligation to point out the dangers of unquestioned allegiance to any cause. We must be better than a charlatan leader of the French Revolution, remembered only for his words: "There go the people; I am their leader; I must follow them."

And the American people have an obligation, too . . . an obligation to exercise their citizenship with a precision that precludes excesses.

I recognize that many of the people who participated in the past Moratorium Day were unaware that its sponsors sought immediate unilateral withdrawal. Perhaps many more had not considered the terrible consequences of immediate unilateral withdrawal.

I hope that all citizens who truly want peace will take the time to read and reflect on the problem. I hope that they will take into consideration the impact of abrupt termination; that they will remember the more than 3,000 innocent men, women, and children slaughtered after the Viet Cong captured Hue last year and the more than 15,000 doctors, nurses, teachers and village leaders murdered by the Viet Cong during the war's early years. The only sin of these people was their desire to build their budding nation of South Vietnam.

A Real Solution

Chanting "Peace Now" is no solution, if "Peace Now" is to permit a wholesale bloodbath. And saying that the President should understand the people's view is no solution. It is time for the people to understand the views of the President they elected to lead them.

First, foreign policy cannot be made in the streets.

Second, turning out a good crowd is not synonymous with turning out a good foreign policy.

Third, the test of a President cannot be reduced to a question of public relations. As the eighteenth-century jurist, Edmund Burke, wrote, "Your representative owes you not his industry only but his judgment; and he betrays instead of serving you, if he sacrifices it to your opinion."

Fourth, the impatience—the understandable frustration over this war—should be focused on the government that is stalling peace while continuing to threaten and invade South Vietnam—and that government's capital is not in Washington. It is in Hanoi.

This was not Richard Nixon's war . . . but it will be Richard Nixon's peace if we only let him make it.

Finally—and most important—regardless of the issue, it is time to stop demonstrating in the streets and start doing something constructive about our institutions. America must recognize the danger of constant carnival. Americans must reckon with irresponsible leadership and reckless words. The mature and sensitive people of this country must realize that their freedom of protest is being exploited by avowed anarchists and communists—yes, I say communist because a member of one of those committees is a member of the communist party and proud of it—who detest everything about this country and want to destroy it.

This is a fact. These are the few . . . these are not necessarily all the leaders. But they prey upon the good intentions of gullible men everywhere. They pervert honest concern to something sick and rancid. They are vultures who sit in trees and watch lions battle, knowing that win, lose or draw, they will be fed.

Abetting the merchants of hate are the parasites of passion. These are the men who value a cause purely for its political mileage. These are the politicians who temporize with the truth by playing both sides to their own advantage. They ooze sympathy for "the cause" but balance each sentence with equally reasoned reservations. Their interest is personal, not moral. They are ideological eunuchs whose most comfortable position is straddling the philosophical fence, soliciting votes from both sides.

Aiding the few who seek to destroy and the many who seek to exploit is a terrifying spirit, the new face of self-righteousness. Former HEW [Department of Health, Education and Welfare] Secretary John Gardner described it: "Sad to say, it's fun to hate . . . that is today's fashion. Rage and hate in a good cause! Be vicious for virtue, self-indulgent for higher purposes, dishonest in the service of a higher honesty."

This is what is happening in this nation . . . we are an effete society if we let it happen here.

I do not overstate the case. If I am aware of the danger, the convicted rapist Eldridge Cleaver is aware of the potential. From his Moscow hotel room he predicted, "Many complacent regimes thought that they would be in power eternally—and awoke one morning to find themselves up against the wall. I expect that to happen in the United States in our lifetimes."

People cannot live in a state of perpetual electric shock. Tired of a convulsive society, they settle for an authoritarian society. As Thomas Hobbes discerned three centuries ago, men will seek the security of a Leviathan state as a comfortable alternative to a life that is "nasty, brutish, and short."

Right now we must decide whether we will take the trouble to stave off a totalitarian state. Will we stop the wildness now before it is too late, before the witch-hunting and repression that are all too inevitable begin?

Will Congress settle down to the issues of the nation and reform the institutions of America as our President asks? Can the press ignore the pipers who lead the parades? Will the heads of great universities protect the rights of all their students? Will parents have the courage to say no to their children? Will people have the intelligence to boycott pornography and violence? Will citizens refuse to be led by a series of Judas goats down tortuous paths of delusion and self-destruction?

Will we defend fifty centuries of accumulated wisdom? For that is our heritage. Will we make the effort to preserve America's bold, successful experiment in truly representative government? Or do we care so little that we will casually toss it all aside?

Because on the eve of our nation's 200th birthday, we have reached the crossroads. Because at this moment totalitarianism's threat does not necessarily have a foreign accent. Because we have a home-grown menace, made and manufactured in the U.S.A. Because if we are lazy or foolish, this nation could forfeit its integrity, never to be free again.

I do not want this to happen to America. And I do not think that you do either. We have something magnificent here . . . something worth fighting for . . . and now is the time for all good men to fight for the soul of their country. Let us stop apologizing for our past. Let us conserve and create for the future.

Dissent Within the Ranks

Robert D. Heinl Jr.

Although most American protest against the Vietnam War took place within the United States, there was a significant antiwar movement within the ranks of those posted, sometimes against their will, in Vietnam. In the following article, which was originally published in the *Armed Forces Journal* in 1971, Colonel Robert D. Heinl Jr., a combat veteran with twenty-seven years experience in the U.S. Marines, offers his view of morale in the American military. According to Heinl, as of 1971 the armed forces of the United States were wracked with problems and a great many troops were unwilling to fight.

As you read, consider the following questions:
1. As used by Heinl, what does the phrase "search and evade" mean?
2. How does Heinl characterize the relationship between military morale and mainstream American society?
3. What is the prevailing public image of the military, according to Heinl?

The morale, discipline and battleworthiness of the U.S. Armed Forces are, with a few salient exceptions, lower and worse than at any time in this century and possibly in the history of the United States.

By every conceivable indicator, our army that now remains in Vietnam is in a state approaching collapse, with individual units avoiding or having refused combat, murdering their officers and noncommissioned officers, drugridden, and dispirited where not near-mutinous.

Robert D. Heinl Jr., "The Collapse of the Armed Forces," *Vietnam and America: A Documented History*, edited by Marvin Gettleman, Jane Franklin, Marilyn Young, and H. Bruce Franklin. New York: Grove Press, 1985. Copyright © 1971 by the Armed Forces Journal. Reproduced by permission.

Elsewhere than Vietnam, the situation is nearly as serious.

Intolerably clobbered and buffeted from without and within by social turbulence, pandemic drug addiction, race war, sedition, civilian scapegoatise, draftee recalcitrance and malevolence, barracks theft and common crime, unsupported in their travail by the general government, in Congress as well as the executive branch, distrusted, disliked, and often reviled by the public, the uniformed services today are places of agony for the loyal, silent professionals who doggedly hang on and try to keep the ship afloat.

The responses of the services to these unheard-of conditions, forces and new public attitudes, are confused, resentful, occasionally pollyanna-ish, and in some cases even calculated to worsen the malaise that is wracking them.

While no senior officer (especially one on active duty) can openly voice any such assessment, the foregoing conclusions find virtually unanimous support in numerous non-attributable interviews with responsible senior and midlevel officers, as well as career noncommissioned officers and petty officers in all services.

Historical precedents do exist for some of the services' problems, such as desertion, mutiny, unpopularity, seditious attacks, and racial troubles. Others, such as drugs, pose difficulties that are wholly new. Nowhere, however, in the history of the Armed Forces have comparable past troubles presented themselves in such general magnitude, acuteness, or concentrated focus as today.

By several orders of magnitude, the Army seems to be in worst trouble. But the Navy has serious and unprecedented problems, while the Air Force, on the surface at least still clear of the quicksands in which the Army is sinking, is itself facing disquieting difficulties.

Only the Marines—who have made the news this year by their hard line against indiscipline and general permissiveness—seem, with their expected staunchness and tough tradition, to be weathering the storm.

To understand the military consequences of what is happening to the U.S. Armed Forces, Vietnam is a good place to start. It is in Vietnam that the rearguard of a 500,000-man army, in its day (and in the observation of the writer) the best army the United States ever put into the field, is numbly extricating itself from a nightmare war the Armed Forces feel they had foisted on them by bright civilians who are now back on campus writing books about the folly of it all.

"They have set up separate companies," writes an American soldier from Cu Chi, quoted in the *New York Times*, "for men who refuse to go out into the field. It is no big thing to refuse to go. If a man is ordered to go to such and such a place he no longer goes through the hassle of refusing; he just packs his shirt and goes to visit some buddies at another base camp. Operations have become incredibly ragtag. Many guys don't even put on their uniforms any more. . . . The American garrisons on the larger bases are virtually disarmed. The lifers have taken our weapons from us and put them under lock and key. . . . There have also been quite a few frag incidents in the battalion."

Can all this really be typical or even truthful?

Unfortunately the answer is yes.

"Frag incidents" or just "fragging" is current soldier slang in Vietnam for the murder or attempted murder of strict, unpopular, or just aggressive officers and NCOs [noncommissioned officers]. With extreme reluctance (after a young West Pointer from Senator Mike Mansfield's Montana was fragged in his sleep) the Pentagon has now disclosed that fraggings in 1970 (209) have more than doubled those of the previous year (96).

Word of the deaths of officers will bring cheers at troop movies or in bivouacs of certain units.

In one such division—the morale-plagued Americal—fraggings during 1971 have been authoritatively estimated to be running about one a week.

Yet fraggings, though hard to document, form part of the ugly lore of every war. The first such verified incident known to have taken place occurred 190 years ago when Pennsylvania soldiers in the Continental Army killed one of their captains during the night of 1 January 1781.

Bounties and Evasions

Bounties, raised by common subscription in amounts running anywhere from $50 to $1,000, have been widely reported put on the heads of leaders whom the privates and Sp4s [specialist fourth class, a rank] want to rub out.

Shortly after the costly assault on Hamburger Hill in mid-1969, the GI underground newspaper in Vietnam, "GI Says," publicly offered a $10,000 bounty on LCol Weldon Honeycutt, the officer who ordered (and led) the attack. Despite several attempts, however, Honeycutt managed to live out his tour and return Stateside.

"Another Hamburger Hill" (i.e., toughly contested assault), conceded a veteran major, "is definitely out."

The issue of "combat refusal," an official euphemism for disobedience of orders to fight—the soldier's gravest crime—has only recently been again precipitated on the frontier of Laos by Troop B, 1st Cavalry's mass refusal to recapture their captain's command vehicle containing communication gear, codes and other secret operation orders.

As early as mid-1969, however, an entire company of the 196th Light Infantry Brigade publicly sat down on the battlefield. Later that year, another rifle company, from the famed 1st Air Cavalry Division, flatly refused—on CBS-TV—to advance down a dangerous trail. . . .

While denying further unit refusals, the Air Cav has admitted some 35 individual refusals in 1970 alone. By comparison, only two years earlier in 1968, the entire number of officially recorded refusals for our whole army in Vietnam—from over seven divisions—was 68.

"Search and evade" (meaning tacit avoidance of combat by units in the field) is now virtually a principle of war, vividly expressed by the GI phrase, "CYA (cover your ass) and get home!"

That "search-and-evade" has not gone unnoticed by the enemy is underscored by the Viet Cong delegation's recent statement at the Paris Peace Talks that communist units in Indochina have been ordered not to engage American units which do not molest them. The same statement boasted—

not without foundation in fact—that American defectors are in the VC ranks.

Symbolic anti-war fasts (such as the one at Pleiku where an entire medical unit, led by its officers, refused Thanksgiving turkey), peace symbols, "V"-signs not for victory but for peace, booing and cursing of officers and even of hapless entertainers such as Bob Hope, are unhappily commonplace.

As for drugs and race, Vietnam's problems today not only reflect but reinforce those of the Armed Forces as a whole. In April, for example, members of a Congressional investigating subcommittee reported that 10 to 15% of our troops in Vietnam are now using high-grade heroin, and that drug addiction there is "of epidemic proportions."

Only last year an Air Force major and command pilot for Ambassador Bunker was apprehended at Tan Son Nhut air base outside Saigon with $8-million worth of heroin in his aircraft. This major is now in Leavenworth [military prison].

Early this year, an Air Force regular colonel was court-martialed and cashiered for leading his squadron in pot parties, while, at Cam Ranh Air Force Base, 43 members of the base security police squadron were recently swept up in dragnet narcotics raids.

All the foregoing facts—and many more dire indicators of the worst kind of military trouble—point to widespread conditions among American forces in Vietnam that have only been exceeded in this century by the French Army's Nivelle mutinies of 1917 and the collapse of the Tsarist armies in 1916 and 1917.

A Mirror of America

It is a truism that national armies closely reflect societies from which they have been raised. It would be strange indeed if the Armed Forces did not today mirror the agonizing divisions and social traumas of American society, and of course they do.

For this very reason, our Armed Forces outside Vietnam not only reflect these conditions but disclose the depths of their troubles in an awful litany of sedition, disaffection, desertion, race, drugs, breakdowns of authority, abandonment of discipline, and, as a cumulative result, the lowest state of military morale in the history of the country.

Sedition—coupled with disaffection within the ranks, and externally fomented with an audacity and intensity previously inconceivable—infests the Armed Services:

• At best count, there appear to be some 144 underground newspapers published on or aimed at U.S. military bases in this country and overseas. Since 1970 the number of such sheets has increased 40% (up from 103 last fall). These journals are not mere gripe-sheets that poke soldier fun in the "Beetle Bailey" tradition, at the brass and the sergeants. "In Vietnam" writes the Ft Lewis–McChord Free Press, "the Lifers, the Brass, are the true Enemy, not the enemy." Another West Coast sheet advises readers: "Don't desert. Go to Vietnam and kill your commanding officer."

• At least 14 GI dissent organizations (including two made up exclusively of officers) now operate more or less openly. Ancillary to these are at least six antiwar veterans' groups which strive to influence GIs.

• Three well-established lawyer groups specialize in support of GI dissent. Two (GI Civil Liberties Defense Committee and New York Draft and Military Law Panel) operate in the open. A third is a semi-underground network of lawyers who can only be contacted through the GI Alliance, a Washington, D.C., group which tries to coordinate seditious antimilitary activities throughout the country.

One antimilitary legal effort operates right in the theater of war. A three-man law office, backed by the Lawyers' Military Defense Committee, of Cambridge, Mass., was set up last fall in Saigon to provide free civilian legal services for dissident soldiers being court-martialed in Vietnam.

Besides these lawyers' fronts, the Pacific Counseling Service (an umbrella organization with Unitarian backing for a prolifery [sic] of antimilitary activities) provides legal help and incitement to dissident GIs through not one but seven branches (Tacoma, Oakland, Los Angeles, San Diego, Monterey, Tokyo, and Okinawa).

Another of Pacific Counseling's activities is to air-drop planeloads of seditious literature into Oakland's sprawling Army Base, our major West Coast staging point for Vietnam.

• On the religious front, a community of turbulent priests and clergymen, some unfrocked, calls itself the Order of Maximilian. Maximilian is a saint said to have been martyred by the Romans for refusing military service as un-Christian. Maximilian's present-day followers visit military posts, infiltrate brigs and stockades in the guise of spiritual counseling, work to recruit military chaplains, and hold services of "consecrations" of post chapels in the name of their saintly draft-dodger.

• By present count at least 11 (some go as high as 26) off-base antiwar "coffee houses" ply GIs with rock music, lukewarm coffee, antiwar literature, how-to-do-it tips on desertion, and similar disruptive counsels. Among the best-known coffee houses are: The Shelter Half (Ft Lewis, Wash.); The Home Front (Ft Carson, Colo.); and The Oleo Strut (Ft Hood, Tex.).

• The nation-wide campus-radical offensive against ROTC and college officer-training is well known. Events last year at Stanford University, however, demonstrate the extremes to which this campaign (which peaked after Cambodia) has gone. After the Stanford faculty voted to accept a modified, specially restructured ROTC program, the university was subjected to a cyclone of continuing violence which included at least $200,000 in ultimate damage to buildings (highlighted by systematic destruction of 40 twenty-foot stained glass windows in the library). In the end, led by university president Richard W. Lyman, the faculty reversed itself. Lyman was quoted at the time that "ROTC is costing Stanford too much.". . .

One militant West Coast Group, Movement for a Democratic Military (MDM), has specialized in weapons theft from military bases in California. During 1970, large armory thefts were successfully perpetrated against Oakland Army Base, Fts Cronkhite and Ord, and even the Marine

Corps Base at Camp Pendleton, where a team wearing marine uniforms got away with nine M-16 rifles and an M-79 grenade launcher.

Operating in the Middle West, three soldiers from Ft Carson, Colo., home of the Army's permissive experimental unit, the 4th Mechanized Division, were recently indicted by federal grand jury for dynamiting the telephone exchange, power plant and water works of another Army installation, Camp McCoy, Wis., on 26 July 1970.

The Navy, particularly on the West Coast, has also experienced disturbing cases of sabotage in the past two years, mainly directed at ships' engineering and electrical machinery.

It will be surprising, according to informed officers, if further such tangible evidence of disaffection within the ranks does not continue to come to light. Their view is that the situation could become considerably worse before it gets better. . . .

One area of the U.S. Government in which the Armed Forces are encountering noticeable lack of support is the federal judiciary. . . .

Part of the defense establishment's problem with the judiciary is the now widely pursued practice of taking commanding officers into civil courts by dissident soldiers either to harass or annul normal discipline or administrative procedures of the services.

Only a short time ago, for example, a dissident group of active-duty officers, members of the Concerned Officers' Movement (COM), filed a sweeping lawsuit against Defense Secretary Laird himself, as well as all three service secretaries, demanding official recognition of their "right" to oppose the Vietnam war, accusing the secretaries of "harassing" them, and calling for court injunction to ban disciplinary "retaliation" against COM members. . . .

Racial Incidents

Sedition and subversion, and legal harassment, rank near the top of what might be called the unprecedented external problems that elements in American society are inflicting on the Armed Forces.

Internally speaking, racial conflicts and drugs—also previously insignificant—are tearing the services apart today. . . .

Racial conflicts (most but not all sparked by young black enlisted men) are erupting murderously in all services.

At a recent high commanders' conference, General [William C.] Westmoreland and other senior generals heard the report from Germany that in many units white soldiers are now afraid to enter barracks alone at night for fear of "head-hunting" ambushes by blacks.

In the quoted words of one soldier on duty in West Germany, "I'm much more afraid of getting mugged on the post than I am of getting attacked by the Russians."

Other reports tell of jail-delivery attacks on Army stockades and military police to release black prisoners, and of officers being struck in public by black soldiers. Augsburg, Krailsheim, and Hohenfels are said to be rife with racial trouble. Hohenfels was the scene of a racial flagging last year—one of the few so far recorded outside Vietnam.

In Ulm, last fall, a white noncommissioned officer killed a black soldier who was holding a loaded .45 on two unarmed white officers.

Elsewhere, according to *Fortune* magazine, junior officers are now being attacked at night when inspecting barracks containing numbers of black soldiers.

Kelley Hill, a Ft Benning, Ga., barracks area, has been the scene of repeated nighttime assaults on white soldiers. One such soldier bitterly remarked, "Kelley Hill may belong to the commander in the daytime but it belongs to the blacks after dark.". . .

But the Army has no monopoly on racial troubles.

As early as July 1969 the Marines (who had previously enjoyed a highly praised record on race) made headlines at Camp Lejeune, N.C., when a mass affray launched by 30–50 black Marines ended fatally with a white corporal's skull smashed in and 15 other white Marines in the sick bay.

That same year, at Newport, R.I., naval station, blacks killed a white petty officer, while in March 1971 the National Naval Medical Center in Bethesda, Md., outside Washington, was beset by racial fighting so severe that the base enlisted men's club had to be closed.

All services are today striving energetically to cool and control this ugly violence which in the words of one non-commissioned officer, has made his once taut unit divide up "like two street gangs.". . .

Drugs and the Military

The drug problem—like the civilian situation from which it directly derives—is running away with the services. In March, Navy Secretary John H. Chafee, speaking for the two sea services, said bluntly that drug abuse in both Navy and Marines is out of control.

In 1966, the Navy discharged 170 drug offenders. Three years later (1969), 3,800 were discharged. Last year in 1970, the total jumped to over 5,000.

Drug abuse in the Pacific Fleet—with Asia on one side, and kinky California on the other—gives the Navy its worst headaches. To cite one example, a destroyer due to sail from the West Coast last year for the Far East nearly had to postpone deployment when, five days before departure, a ring of some 30 drug users (over 10 percent of the crew) was uncovered.

Only last week, eight midshipmen were dismissed from the Naval Academy following disclosure of an alleged drug ring. While the Navy emphatically denies allegations in a copyrighted article by the *Annapolis Capitol* that up to 1,000 midshipmen now use marijuana, midshipman sources confirm that pot is anything but unknown at Annapolis.

Yet the Navy is somewhat ahead in the drug game because of the difficulty in concealing addiction at close quarters aboard ship, and because fixes are unobtainable during long deployments at sea.

The Air Force, despite 2,715 drug investigations in 1970, is in even better shape: its rate of 3 cases per thousand airmen is the lowest in the services.

By contrast, the Army had 17,742 drug investigations

the same year. According to Col Thomas B. Hauschild, of the Medical Command of our Army forces in Europe, some 46 percent of the roughly 200,000 soldiers there had used illegal drugs at least once. In one battalion surveyed in West Germany, over 50 percent of the men smoked marijuana regularly (some on duty), while roughly half of those were using hard drugs of some type.

What those statistics say is that the Armed Forces (like their parent society) are in the grip of a drug pandemic—a conclusion underscored by the one fact that, just since 1968, the total number of verified drug addiction cases throughout the Armed Forces has nearly doubled. One other yardstick: according to military medical sources, needle hepatitis now poses as great a problem among young soldiers as VD [venereal disease].

At Ft Bragg, the Army's third largest post, adjacent to Fayetteville, N.C. (a garrison town whose conditions one official likened to New York's "East Village" and San Francisco's "Haight-Ashbury") a recent survey disclosed that 4% (or over 1,400) of the 36,000 soldiers there are hard-drug (mainly heroin and LSD) addicts. In the 82nd Airborne Division, the strategic-reserve unit that boasts its title of "America's Honor Guard," approximately 450 soldier drug abusers were being treated when this reporter visited the post in April. About a hundred were under intensive treatment in special drug wards. . . .

Desertions and Disasters

With conditions what they are in the Armed Forces, and with intense efforts on the part of elements in our society to disrupt discipline and destroy morale the consequences can be clearly measured in two ultimate indicators: manpower retention (reenlistments and their antithesis, desertions); and the state of discipline.

In both respects the picture is anything but encouraging. . . .

Desertion rates are going straight up in Army, Marines, and Air Force. Curiously, however, during the period since

1968 when desertion has nearly doubled for all three other services, the Navy's rate has risen by less than 20 percent.

In 1970, the Army had 65,643 deserters, or roughly the equivalent of four infantry divisions. This desertion rate (52.3 soldiers per thousand) is well over twice the peak rate for Korea (22.5 per thousand). It is more than quadruple the 1966 desertion-rate (14.7 per thousand) of the then well-trained, high-spirited professional Army.

If desertions continue to rise (as they are still doing this year), they will attain or surpass the WWII peak of 63 per thousand, which, incidentally, occurred in the same year (1945) when more soldiers were actually being discharged from the Army for psychoneurosis than were drafted.

The Air Force—relatively uninvolved in the Vietnam war, all-volunteer, management-oriented rather than disciplinary and hierarchic—enjoys a numerical rate of less than one deserter per thousand men, but even this is double what it was three years ago.

The Marines in 1970 had the highest desertion index in the modern history of the Corps and, for that year at least, slightly higher than the Army's. As the Marines now phase out of Vietnam (and haven't taken a draftee in nearly two years), their desertions are expected to decrease sharply. Meanwhile, grimly remarked one officer, "Let the bastards go. We're all the better without them."

Letting the bastards go is something the Marines can probably afford. "The Marine Corps Isn't Looking for a Lot of Recruits," reads a current recruiting poster, "We Just Need a Few Good Men." This is the happy situation of a Corps slimming down to an elite force again composed of true volunteers who want to be professionals.

But letting the bastards go doesn't work at all for the Army and the Navy, who do need a lot of recruits and whose reenlistment problems are dire.

Admiral Elmo R. Zumwalt, Jr, Chief of Naval Operations, minces no words, "We have a personnel crisis," he recently said, "that borders on disaster."

The Navy's crisis, as Zumwalt accurately describes it, is

that of a highly technical, material oriented service that finds itself unable to retain the expensively-trained technicians needed to operate warships, which are the largest, most complex items of machinery that man makes and uses.

Avoiding Danger

If 45% of his sailors shipped over after their first enlistment, Admiral Zumwalt would be all smiles. With only 13% doing so, he is growing sideburns to enhance the Navy's appeal to youth.

Among the Army's volunteer (non-draftee) soldiers on their first hitch, the figures are much the same: less than 14% re-up.

The Air Force is slightly, but not much, better off: 16% of its first-termers stay on.

Moreover—and this is the heart of the Army's dilemma—only 4% of the voluntary enlistees now choose service in combat arms (infantry, armor, artillery) and of those only 2.5% opt for infantry. Today's soldiers, it seems, volunteer readily enough for the tail of the Army, but not for its teeth.

For all services, the combined retention rate this past year is about half what it was in 1966, and the lowest since the bad times of similar low morale and national disenchantment after Korea.

Both Army and Navy are responding to their manpower problems in measures intended to seduce recruits and reenlistees: disciplinary permissiveness, abolition of reveille and KP [kitchen police], fewer inspections, longer haircuts—essentially cosmetic changes aimed at softening (and blurring) traditional military and naval images. . . .

The trouble of the services—produced by and also in turn producing the dismaying conditions described in this article—is above all a crisis of soul and backbone. It entails—the word is not too strong—something very near a collapse of the command authority and leadership George Washington saw as the soul of military forces. This collapse results, at least in part, from a concurrent collapse of public confidence in the military establishment.

General Matthew B. Ridgway, one of the Army's finest leaders in this century (who revitalized the shaken Eighth Army in Korea after its headlong rout by the Chinese in 1950) recently said, "Not before in my lifetime . . . has the Army's public image fallen to such low esteem. . . ."

But the fall in public esteem of all three major services—not just the Army—is exceeded by the fall or at least the enfeeblement of the hierarchic and disciplinary system by which they exist and, when ordered to do so, fight and sometimes die.

CHAPTER

5

SEEKING PEACE

CHAPTER PREFACE

For nearly twenty years following the Geneva Convention of 1954, the overriding goal of American policy in Vietnam was to prevent the Communists from controlling South Vietnam. Initially, the United States hoped money and military advisers would be enough, but by 1965 it was conducting regular bombing runs of North Vietnam and shipping American troops overseas into combat positions. Although it battled both the North Vietnamese Army (NVA), and the Vietcong guerrilla army supported by the North, the United States never tried to invade and occupy North Vietnam. This would have greatly increased American casualties and provoked China, a nuclear power with a massive army of its own. Thus, the only way for America to prevent the Communist takeover of South Vietnam was to somehow convince the Communists, whether they were North Vietnamese or Vietcong, to abandon the goal of a united Vietnam under Communist rule.

Initially, the United States hoped to convince the Communists to capitulate by inflicting heavy damage, especially through bombing campaigns. In 1965, for instance, bombing campaigns were twice put on hold in the hope that the NVA and the Vietcong would use the pause in bombing to negotiate for peace. This tactic failed, however, and in time the levels of American troop commitment grew, as did casualties on both sides. By the end of 1965, 184,300 American troops were in Vietnam. This number jumped to 389,000 by the end of 1966 and then to around 500,000 in 1967, where it remained throughout 1968. At the same time, the total number of American soldiers killed grew from 5,000 in 1966 to approximately 30,000 by the end of 1968. By the spring of 1968, it was obvious to Americans that the war was not going well and that peace was proving elusive.

In late March 1968 President Lyndon Johnson announced

that he would not seek reelection, a decision that followed the resignation of Defense Secretary Robert McNamara by just a few months. Johnson also hinted that he would enter negotiations with the Communists and began secret meetings with the Vietnamese in Paris. Although word of the negotiations soon became public, the Democrats were not able to salvage the presidency in the 1968 election, and Johnson was replaced by Republican Richard Nixon, who said he had a plan to end the war.

Nixon's plan called for the "Vietnamization" of the war. From the onset of hostilities, both American troops and South Vietnamese soldiers had battled the Communists. Nixon pledged, however, to increase aerial bombardment of North Vietnam while gradually withdrawing American ground forces and shifting the burden of the land war onto the South Vietnamese army. Although U.S. troop levels reached their highest point in April 1969—543,000—by the end of the year Nixon had sent 85,000 soldiers home. By the end of 1970, American troop levels had dropped to 280,000, and by the end of 1971, just 150,000 American soldiers remained in Vietnam. The last U.S. combat troops left Vietnam in 1972.

The reduction in American ground troops coincided with an increase in American bombing raids against North Vietnam. Between 1970 and 1973 the air war expanded, with both Hanoi and Haiphong, North Vietnam's two largest cities, being targeted in December 1972. The increased aerial bombardment, and especially the raids against cities, were unpopular in the United States and drew condemnation from the international community. Finally, in January 1973, the United States, North Vietnam, South Vietnam, and the Vietcong signed the Paris Peace Accords, which ended American involvement but left Vietnam divided and at war.

The Nixon administration had secured the agreement of the South Vietnamese government by pledging it would not abandon South Vietnam, but the pledge proved impossible to fulfill. In June 1973 the U.S. Congress forbade any further American military action in Southeast Asia, making it clear that henceforth South Vietnam was on its own. The South Vietnamese regime managed to fend off Communist forces for nearly two more years, but on April 30, 1975, the Vietcong took control of Saigon, the capital of South Vietnam, and the South Vietnamese government offered its unconditional surrender. The documents in this chapter explore the search for the peace that had come at last.

Peace Will Be Elusive

Hans J. Morgenthau

When the following article was originally published in the *New York Times Magazine* in April 1965, the eight-year-long American air campaign against North Vietnam had just begun. The author of the article, Hans J. Morgenthau, analyzes the goals articulated by President Lyndon Johnson in a speech at Johns Hopkins University on April 7, 1965, and discusses various challenges on the road to peace. Morgenthau was widely regarded as the preeminent American scholar of international relations.

As you read, consider the following questions:
1. Why does Morgenthau think the policy of containment will not work against communism in Asia?
2. How does Morgenthau propose the United States extricate itself from the war in Vietnam?
3. What criticism does Morgenthau make of the American emphasis on North Vietnam?

The address which President Johnson delivered on April 7 [1965] at Johns Hopkins University is important for two reasons. On the one hand, the President has shown for the first time a way out of the impasse in which we find ourselves in Vietnam. By agreeing to negotiations without preconditions he has opened the door to negotiations which those preconditions had made impossible from the outset.

By proposing a project for the economic development of Southeast Asia—with North Vietnam a beneficiary and the Soviet Union a supporter—he has implicitly recognized the variety of national interests in the Communist world and the need for varied American responses tailored to those interests. By asking "that the people of South Vietnam be allowed to guide their own country in their own way," he has left all possibilities open for the future evolution of relations between North and South Vietnam.

On the other hand, the President reiterated the intellectual assumptions and policy proposals which brought us to an impasse and which make it impossible to extricate ourselves. The President has linked our involvement in Vietnam with our war of independence and has proclaimed the freedom of all nations as the goal of our foreign policy. He has started from the assumption that there are two Vietnamese nations, one of which has attacked the other, and he sees that attack as an integral part of unlimited Chinese aggression. Consistent with this assumption, the President is willing to negotiate with China and North Vietnam but not with the Vietcong [Communist revolutionaries within South Vietnam].

Yet we cannot have it both ways. We cannot at the same time embrace these false assumptions and pursue new sound policies. Thus we are faced with a real dilemma. This dilemma is by no means of the President's making.

Containing Communism

We are militarily engaged in Vietnam by virtue of a basic principle of our foreign policy that was implicit in the Truman Doctrine of 1947 and was put into practice by [Secretary of State] John Foster Dulles from 1954 onward. This principle is the military containment of Communism. Containment had its origins in Europe. Dulles applied it to the Middle East and Asia through a series of bilateral and multilateral alliances. Yet what was an outstanding success in Europe turned out to be a dismal failure elsewhere. The reasons for that failure are twofold.

First, the threat that faced the nations of Western Europe in the aftermath of the Second World War was primarily military. It was the threat of the Red [Soviet] Army marching westward. Behind the line of military demarcation of

1945 which the policy of containment declared to be the western-most limit of the Soviet empire, there was an ancient civilization, only temporarily weak and able to maintain itself against the threat of Communist subversion.

The situation is different in the Middle East and Asia. The threat there is not primarily military but political in nature. Weak governments and societies provide opportunities for Communist subversion. Military containment is irrelevant to that threat and may even be counter productive. Thus the Baghdad Pact did not protect Egypt from Soviet influence and SEATO [South East Asia Treaty Organization] has had no bearing on Chinese influence in Indonesia and Pakistan.

Second, and more important, even if China were threatening her neighbors primarily by military means, it would be impossible to contain her by erecting a military wall at the periphery of her empire. For China is, even in her present underdeveloped state, the dominant power in Asia. She is this by virtue of the quality and quantity of her population, her geographic position, her civilization, her past power remembered and her future power anticipated. Anybody who has traveled in Asia with his eyes and ears open must have been impressed by the enormous impact which the resurgence of China has made upon all manner of men, regardless of class and political conviction, from Japan to Pakistan.

The issue China poses is political and cultural predominance. The United States can no more contain Chinese influence in Asia by arming South Vietnam and Thailand than China could contain American influence in the Western Hemisphere by arming, say, Nicaragua and Costa Rica.

If we are convinced that we cannot live with a China predominant on the mainland of Asia, then we must strike at the heart of Chinese power—that is, rather than try to contain the power of China, we must try to destroy that power itself. Thus there is logic on the side of that small group of Americans who are convinced that war between the United States and China is inevitable and that the earlier that war comes, the better will be the chances for the United States to win it.

Yet, while logic is on their side, practical judgment is against them. For while China is obviously no match for the United States in overall power, China is largely immune to the specific types of power in which the superiority of the United States consisted—that is nuclear, air and naval power. Certainly, the United States has the power to destroy the nuclear installations and the major industrial and population centers of China, but this destruction would not defeat China; it would only set her development back. To be defeated, China has to be conquered.

Physical conquest would require the deployment of millions of American soldiers on the mainland of Asia. No American military leader has ever advocated a course of action so fraught with incalculable risks, so uncertain of outcome, requiring sacrifices so out of proportion to the interests at stake and the benefits to be expected. President [Dwight] Eisenhower declared on Feb. 10, 1954, that he "could conceive of no greater tragedy than for the United States to become involved in an all-out war in Indochina." General [Douglas] MacArthur, in the Congressional hearings concerning his dismissal and in personal conversation with President [John F.] Kennedy, emphatically warned against sending American foot soldiers to the Asian mainland to fight China.

Accepting China

If we do not want to set ourselves goals which cannot be attained with the means we are willing to employ, we must learn to accommodate ourselves to the predominance of China on the Asian mainland. It is instructive to note that those Asian nations which have done so—such as Burma and Cambodia—live peacefully in the shadow of the Chinese giant.

This *modus vivendi*, composed of legal independence and various degrees of actual dependence, has indeed been for more than a millennium the persistent pattern of Chinese predominance on the mainland of Asia. The military conquest of Tibet is the sole exception to that pattern. The military operations at the Indian border do not diverge from it, since their purpose was the establishment of a frontier disputed by both sides.

On the other hand, those Asian nations which have allowed themselves to be transformed into outposts of American military power—such as Laos a few years ago, South Vietnam and Thailand—have become the actual or prospective victims of Communist aggression and subversion. Thus it appears that peripheral military containment is counterproductive. Challenged at its periphery by American military power at its weakest—that is, by the proxy of client-states—China or its proxies respond with locally superior military and political power.

In specific terms, accommodation means four things: (1) recognition of the political and cultural predominance of China on the mainland of Asia as a fact of life; (2) liquidation of the peripheral military containment of China; (3) strengthening of the uncommitted nations of Asia by non-military means; (4) assessment of Communist governments in Asia in terms not of Communist doctrine but of their relation to the interests and power of the United States.

Getting Out of Vietnam

In the light of these principles, the alternative to our present policies in Vietnam would be this: a face-saving agreement which would allow us to disengage ourselves militarily in stages spaced in time; restoration of the status quo of the Geneva Agreement of 1954, with special emphasis upon all-Vietnamese elections; cooperation with the Soviet Union in support of a Titoist [referring to Yugoslavian president Tito, whose Communist policies were independent of, and sometimes countered, those of the Soviet Union] all-Vietnamese Government which would be likely to emerge from such elections.

This last point is crucial, for our present policies not only drive Hanoi into the waiting arms of Peking, but also make it very difficult for Moscow to pursue an independent policy. Our interests in Southeast Asia are identical with those of the Soviet Union: to prevent the expansion of the *military* power of China. But while our present policies invite that expansion, so do they make it impossible for the Soviet Union to join us in preventing it. If we were to reconcile ourselves to the establishment of a Titoist government in all of Vietnam, the Soviet Union could successfully compete with China in claiming credit for it and surreptitiously cooperate with us in maintaining it.

Testing the President's proposals by these standards, one realizes how far they go in meeting them. These proposals do not preclude a return to the Geneva agreement and even assume the existence of a Titoist government in North Vietnam. Nor do they preclude the establishment of a Titoist government for all of Vietnam; provided the people of South Vietnam have freely agreed to it. They also envision the active participation of the Soviet Union in establishing and maintaining a new balance of power in Southeast Asia. On the other hand, the President has flatly rejected a withdrawal "under the cloak of a meaningless agreement." The controlling word is obviously "meaningless," and only the future can tell whether we shall consider any face-saving agreement as "meaningless" regardless of its political context.

A False Dichotomy

However, we are under a psychological compulsion to continue our military presence in South Vietnam as part of the peripheral military containment of China. We have been emboldened in this course of action by the identification of the enemy as "Communist," seeing in every Communist party and regime an extension of hostile Russian or Chinese power. This identification was justified 20 or 15 years ago when Communism still had a monolithic character. Here, as elsewhere, our modes of thought and action have been rendered obsolete by new developments.

It is ironic that this simple juxtaposition of "Communism" and "free world" was erected by John Foster Dulles's crusading moralism into the guiding principle of American foreign policy at a time when the national communism of Yugoslavia, the neutralism of the third world and the incipient split between the Soviet Union and China were rendering that juxtaposition invalid.

Today, it is belaboring the obvious to say that we are faced not with one monolithic Communism whose uniform hostility must be countered with equally uniform hostility, but with a number of different Communisms whose hostilities, determined by different national interests, vary. In fact, the United States encounters today less hostility from Tito, who is a Communist, than from [Charles] de Gaulle [leader of France], who is not.

We can today distinguish four different types of Communism in view of the kind and degree of hostility to the United States they represent: a Communism identified with the Soviet Union—e.g., Poland; a Communism identified with China—e.g. Albania; a Communism that straddles the fence between the Soviet Union and China—e.g., Rumania, and independent Communism—e.g., Yugoslavia. Each of these Communisms must be dealt with in terms of the bearing its foreign policy has upon the interests of the United States in a concrete instance.

It would, of course, be absurd to suggest that the officials responsible for the conduct of American foreign policy are unaware of these distinctions and of the demands they make for discriminating subtlety. Yet it is an obvious fact of experience that these officials are incapable of living up to these demands when they deal with Vietnam.

Thus they maneuver themselves into a position which is antirevolutionary per se and which requires military opposition to revolution wherever it is found in Asia, regardless of how it affects the interests—and how susceptible it is to the power—of the United States. There is a historic precedent for this kind of policy: [Prince Klemens von] Metternich's military opposition to liberalism after the Napoleonic Wars, which collapsed in 1848. For better or for worse, we live again in an age of revolution. It is the task of statesmanship not to oppose what cannot be opposed with a chance of success, but to bend it to one's own interests. This is what the President is trying to do with his proposal for the economic development of Southeast Asia.

Why do we support the Saigon Government in the civil war against the Vietcong? Because the Saigon Government is "free" and the Vietcong are "Communist." By containing Vietnamese Communism, we assume that we are really containing the Communism of China.

Yet this assumption is at odds with the historic experience of a millennium and is unsupported by contemporary evidence. China is the hereditary enemy of Vietnam, and Ho Chi Minh will become the leader of a Chinese satellite only if the United States forces him to become one.

Furthermore, Ho Chi Minh, like Tito and unlike the Communist governments of the other states of Eastern Europe, came to power not by courtesy of another Communist nation's victorious army but at the head of a victorious army of his own. He is, then, a natural candidate to become an Asian Tito, and the question we must answer is: How adversely would a Titoist Ho Chi Minh, governing all of Vietnam, affect the interests of the United States? The answer can only be: not at all. One can even maintain the proposition that, far from affecting adversely the interests of the United States, it would be in the interest of the United States if the western periphery of China were ringed by a chain of independent states, though they would, of course, in their policies take due account of the predominance of their powerful neighbor.

The Diem Government

The roots of the Vietnamese civil war go back to the very beginning of South Vietnam as an independent state. When President Ngo Dinh Diem took office in 1954, he presided not over a state but over one-half of a country arbitrarily and, in the intentions of all concerned, temporarily severed from the other half. He was generally regarded as a caretaker who would establish the rudiments of an administration until the country was united by nationwide elections to be held in 1956 in accordance with the Geneva accords.

Diem was confronted at home with a number of private armies which were politically, religiously or criminally oriented. To the general surprise, he subdued one after another and created what looked like a viable government. Yet in the process of creating it, he also laid the foundations for the present civil war. He ruthlessly suppressed all opposition, established concentration camps, organized a brutal secret police, closed newspapers and rigged elections. These policies inevitably led to a polarization of the politics of South Vietnam—on one side, Diem's family, surrounded by a Pretorian guard; on the other, the Vietnamese people, backed by the Communists, declaring themselves liberators from foreign domination and internal oppression.

Thus, the possibility of civil war was inherent in the very nature of the Diem regime. It became inevitable after Diem refused to agree to all-Vietnamese elections and, in the face of mounting popular alienation, accentuated the tyrannical aspects of his regime. The South Vietnamese who cherished freedom could not help but oppose him. Threatened by the secret police, they went either abroad or underground where the Communists were waiting for them.

Until the end of last February [1965] the Government of the United States started from the assumption that the war in South Vietnam was a civil war, aided and abetted—but not created—from abroad, and spokesmen for the Government have made time and again the point that the key to winning the war was political and not military and was to be found in South Vietnam itself. It was supposed to lie in transforming the indifference or hostility of the great mass of the South Vietnamese people into positive loyalty to the Government.

To that end, a new theory of warfare called "counterinsurgency" was put into practice. Strategic hamlets were established, massive propaganda campaigns were embarked upon, social and economic measures were at least sporadically taken. But all was to no avail. The mass of the population remained indifferent, if not hostile, and large units of the army ran away or went over to the enemy.

The reasons for this failure are of general significance, for they stem from a deeply ingrained habit of the American mind. We like to think of social problems as technically self-sufficient and susceptible of simple, clear-cut solutions. We tend to think of foreign aid as a kind of self-sufficient, technical economic enterprise subject to the laws of economics and divorced from politics, and of war as a similarly self-sufficient, technical enterprise, to be won as quickly, as cheaply, as thoroughly as possible and divorced from the foreign policy that preceded and is to follow it. Thus our military theoreticians and practitioners conceive of counterinsurgency as though it were just another branch of warfare like artillery or chemical warfare, to be taught in special schools and applied with technical proficiency wherever the occasion arises.

The War We Fight

This view derives of course from a complete misconception of the nature of civil war. People fight and die in civil wars because they have a faith which appears to them worth fighting and dying for, and they can be opposed with a chance of success only by people who have at least as strong a faith.

[Filipino secretary of defense Ramón] Magsaysay could subdue the Huk rebellion in the Philippines because his charisma, proven in action, aroused a faith superior to that of his opponents. In South Vietnam there is nothing to oppose the faith of the Vietcong and, in consequence, the Saigon Government and we are losing the civil war.

A guerrilla war cannot be won without the active support of the indigenous population, short of the physical extermination of that population. Germany was at least consistent when, during the Second World War, faced with unmanageable guerrilla warfare throughout occupied Europe, she tried to master the situation through a deliberate policy of extermination. The French tried "counterinsurgency" in Algeria and failed; 400,000 French troops fought the guerrillas in Indochina for nine years and failed.

The United States has recognized that it is failing in South Vietnam. But it has drawn from this recognition of failure a most astounding conclusion.

The United States has decided to change the character of the war by unilateral declaration from a South Vietnamese civil war to a war of "foreign aggression." "Aggression from the North: The Record of North Vietnam's Campaign to Conquer South Vietnam" is the title of a white paper published by the Department of State on the last day of February, 1965. While normally foreign and military policy is based upon intelligence—that is, the objective assessment of facts— the process is here reversed: a new policy has been decided upon, and intelligence must provide the facts to justify it.

The United States, stymied in South Vietnam and on the verge of defeat, decided to carry the war to North Vietnam not so much in order to retrieve the fortunes of war as to lay the groundwork for "negotiations from strength." In order to justify that new policy, it was necessary to prove that North Vietnam is the real enemy. It is the white paper's purpose to present that proof.

Let it be said right away that the white paper is a dismal failure. The discrepancy between its assertions and the factual evidence adduced to support them borders on the grotesque. It does nothing to disprove, and tends even to confirm, what until the end of February had been official American doctrine: that the main body of the Vietcong is composed of South Vietnamese and that 80 per cent to 90 per cent of their weapons are of American origin.

This document is most disturbing in that it provides a particularly glaring instance of the tendency to conduct foreign and military policy not on their own merits, but as exercises in public relations. The Government fashions an imaginary world that pleases it, and then comes to believe in the reality of that world and acts as though it were real.

It is for this reason that public officials are so resentful of the reporters assigned to Vietnam and have tried to shut them off from the sources of news and even to silence them. They resent the confrontation of their policies with the facts. Yet the facts are what they are, and they take terrible vengeance on those who disregard them.

However, the white paper is but the latest instance of a delusionary tendency which has led American policy in Vietnam astray in other respects. We call the American troops in Vietnam "advisers" and have assigned them by and large to advisory functions, and we have limited the activities of the marines who have now landed in Vietnam to guarding American installations. We have done this for reasons of public relations in order to spare ourselves the odium of open belligerency.

There is an ominous similarity between this technique and that applied to the expedition in the Bay of Pigs. We wanted to overthrow [Cuban dictator Fidel] Castro, but for reasons of public relations we did not want to do it ourselves. So it was not done at all, and our prestige was damaged far beyond what it would have suffered had we worked openly and singlemindedly for the goal we had set ourselves.

Our very presence in Vietnam is in a sense dictated by considerations of public relations: we are afraid lest our prestige would suffer were we to retreat from an untenable position.

One may ask whether we have gained prestige by being involved in a civil war on the mainland of Asia and by being unable to win it. Would we gain more by being unable to extricate ourselves from it, and by expanding it unilaterally into an international war? Is French prestige lower today than it was 11 years ago when France was fighting in Indochina, or five years ago when she was fighting in Algeria? Does not a great power gain prestige by mustering the wisdom and courage necessary to liquidate a losing enterprise? In other words, is it not the mark of greatness, in circumstances such as these, to be able to afford to be indifferent to one's prestige?

The peripheral military containment of China, the indiscriminate crusade against Communism, counterinsurgency as a technically self-sufficient new branch of warfare, the conception of foreign and military policy as a branch of public relations—they are all misconceptions that conjure up terrible dangers for those who base their policies on them.

One can only hope and pray that the vaunted pragmatism and common sense of the American mind—of which the President's new proposals may well be a manifestation—will act as a corrective upon those misconceptions before they lead us from the blind alley in which we find ourselves today to the rim of the abyss. Beyond the present crisis, however, one must hope that the confrontation between these misconceptions and reality will teach us a long-overdue lesson—to rid ourselves of these misconceptions altogether.

A Halt of Bombing Will Lead to Peace

Lyndon Johnson

In late March 1968, amid ongoing antiwar protests and general unhappiness within the United States about the progress of the war, President Lyndon Johnson announced that he would not seek reelection in that year's presidential election. In late October, shortly before the election, Johnson announced in a national address that he had ordered a halt to the bombing of North Vietnam. In this speech, reprinted below, Johnson argues that the cessation of bombing is a signal of the administration's faith in the Paris peace talks, which had begun secretly in May.

As you read, consider the following questions:
1. According to Johnson, what controlled the timing of the American bombing halt?
2. What factors does Johnson suggest might have been responsible for progress in the Paris peace talks?
3. Does Johnson make any predictions about when the war might end?

I speak to you this evening about very important developments in our search for peace in Vietnam.

We have been engaged in discussions with the North Vietnamese in Paris since last May [1968]. The discussions began after I announced on the evening of March 31st in a television speech to the Nation that the United States—in an effort to get talks started on a settlement of the Vietnam war—had stopped the bombing of North Vietnam in the

Lyndon Johnson, address to the nation, October 21, 1968.

area where 90 percent of the people live.

When our representatives—Ambassador [Averell] Harriman and Ambassador [Cyrus] Vance—were sent to Paris, they were instructed to insist throughout the discussions that the legitimate elected Government of South Vietnam must take its place in any serious negotiations affecting the future of South Vietnam.

Therefore, our Ambassadors Harriman and Vance made it abundantly clear to the representatives of North Vietnam in the beginning that—as I had indicated on the evening of March 31st—we would stop the bombing of North Vietnamese territory entirely when that would lead to prompt and productive talks, meaning by that talks in which the Government of Vietnam was free to participate.

Our ambassadors also stressed that we could not stop the bombing so long as by doing so we would endanger the lives and the safety of our troops.

For a good many weeks, there was no movement in the talks at all. The talks appeared to really be deadlocked.

Then a few weeks ago, they entered a new and a very much more hopeful phase.

As we moved ahead, I conducted a series of very intensive discussions with our allies, and with the senior military and diplomatic officers of the United States Government, on the prospects for peace. The President also briefed our congressional leaders and all of the presidential candidates.

Last Sunday evening [October 27, 1968], and throughout Monday, we began to get confirmation of the essential understanding that we had been seeking with the North Vietnamese on the critical issues between us for some time. I spent most of all day Tuesday reviewing every single detail of this matter with our field commander, General [Creighton] Abrams, whom I had ordered home, and who arrived here at the White House at 2:30 in the morning and went into immediate conference with the President and the appropriate members of his Cabinet. We received General Abrams' judgment and we heard his recommendations at some length.

Now, as a result of all of these developments, I have now

ordered that all air, naval, and artillery bombardment of North Vietnam cease as of 8 A.M., Washington time, Friday morning.

I have reached this decision on the basis of the developments in the Paris talks.

And I have reached it in the belief that this action can lead to progress toward a peaceful settlement of the Vietnamese war.

I have already informed the three presidential candidates, as well as the congressional leaders of both the Republican and the Democratic Parties, of the reasons that the Government has made this decision.

A Safe Move

This decision very closely conforms to the statements that I have made in the past concerning a bombing cessation.

It was on August 19th that the President said: "This administration does not intend to move further until it has good reason to believe that the other side intends seriously"—seriously—"to join us in deescalating the war and moving seriously toward peace."

And then again on September 10th, I said: "The bombing will not stop until we are confident that it will not lead to an increase in American casualties."

The Joint Chiefs of Staff, all military men, have assured me—and General Abrams very firmly asserted to me on Tuesday in that early, 2:30 A.M. meeting—that in their military judgment this action should be taken now, and this action would not result in any increase in American casualties.

A regular session of the Paris talks is going to take place next Wednesday, November 6th, at which the representatives of the Government of South Vietnam are free to participate. We are informed by the representatives of the Hanoi Government that the representatives of the National Liberation Front will also be present. I emphasize that their attendance in no way involves recognition of the National Liberation Front in any form. Yet, it conforms to the statements that we have made many times over the years that

President Lyndon Johnson greets American troops in Vietnam in 1966.

the NLF would have no difficulty making its views known.

But what we now expect—what we have a right to expect—are prompt, productive, serious, and intensive negotiations in an atmosphere that is conducive to progress.

We have reached the stage where productive talks can begin. We have made clear to the other side that such talks cannot continue if they take military advantage of them. We cannot have productive talks in an atmosphere where the cities are being shelled and where the demilitarized zone is being abused.

I think I should caution you, my fellow Americans, that arrangements of this kind are never foolproof. For that matter, even formal treaties are never foolproof, as we have learned from our experience.

But in the light of the progress that has been made in recent weeks, and after carefully considering and weighing the unanimous military and diplomatic advice and judgment rendered to the Commander in Chief, I have finally decided to take this step now and to really determine the good faith of those who have assured us that progress will result when bombing ceases and to try to ascertain if an early peace is possible. The overriding consideration that governs us at this hour is the chance and the opportunity that we might have to save human lives, save human lives on both sides of the conflict. Therefore, I have concluded that we should see if they are acting in good faith.

We could be misled—and we are prepared for such a contingency. We pray God it does not occur.

But it should be clear to all of us that the new phase of negotiations which opens on November 6th does not—repeat, does not—mean that a stable peace has yet come to Southeast Asia. There may well be very hard fighting ahead. Certainly, there is going to be some very hard negotiating, because many difficult and critically important issues are still facing these negotiators. But I hope and I believe that with good will we can solve them. We know that negotiations can move swiftly if the common intent of the negotiators is peace in the world.

The world should know that the American people bitterly remember the long, agonizing Korean negotiations of 1951 through 1953—and that our people will just not accept deliberate delay and prolonged procrastination again.

Well then, how has it come about that now, on November 1st, we have agreed to stop the bombardment of North Vietnam?

I would have given all I possess if the conditions had permitted me to stop it months ago; if there had just been any movement in the Paris talks that would have justified me in saying to you, "Now it can be safely stopped."

But I, the President of the United States, do not control the timing of the events in Hanoi. The decisions in Hanoi really determine when and whether it would be possible for us to stop the bombing.

The Role of South Vietnam

We could not retract our insistence on the participation of the Government of South Vietnam in serious talks affecting the future of their people—the people of South Vietnam. For though we have allied with South Vietnam for many years in this struggle, we have never assumed and we shall never demand the role of dictating the future of the people of South Vietnam. The very principle for which we are engaged in South Vietnam—the principle of self-determination—requires that the South Vietnamese people themselves be permitted to freely speak for themselves at the Paris talks and that the South Vietnamese delegation play a leading role in accordance with our agreement with President Nguyen Van Thieu at Honolulu.

It was made just as clear to North Vietnam that a total bombing halt must not risk the lives of our men.

When I spoke last March 31st, I said that evening: "Whether a complete bombing halt becomes possible in the future will be determined by events."

Well, I cannot tell you tonight specifically in all detail why there has been progress in Paris. But I can tell you that a series of hopeful events has occurred in South Vietnam:

—The Government of South Vietnam has grown steadily stronger.

—South Vietnam's Armed Forces have been substantially increased to the point where a million men are tonight under arms, and the effectiveness of these men has steadily improved.

—The superb performance of our own men, under the brilliant leadership of General [William] Westmoreland and General Abrams, has produced truly remarkable results.

Now, perhaps some or all of these factors played a part in bringing about progress in the talks. And when at last progress did come, I believe that my responsibilities to the brave men—our men—who bear the burden of battle in South Vietnam tonight, and my duty to seek an honorable settlement of the war, required me to recognize and required me to act without delay.

I have acted tonight.

Determination and Patience
There have been many long days of waiting for new steps toward peace—days that began in hope, only to end at

night in disappointment. Constancy to our national purpose—which is to seek the basis for a durable peace in
Southeast Asia—has sustained me in all of these hours when
there seemed to be no progress whatever in these talks.

But now that progress has come, I know that your
prayers are joined with mine and with those of all humanity, that the action I announce tonight will be a major step
toward a firm and an honorable peace in Southeast Asia. It
can be.

So, what is required of us in these new circumstances is
exactly that steady determination and patience which has
brought us to this more hopeful prospect.

What is required of us is a courage and a steadfastness,
and a perseverance here at home, that will match that of
our men who fight for us tonight in Vietnam.

So, I ask you not only for your prayers but for the courageous and understanding support that Americans always
give their President and their leader in an hour of trial. With
that understanding, and with that support, we shall not fail.

Seven months ago I said that I would not permit the
Presidency to become involved in the partisan divisions
that were then developing in this political year. Accordingly, on the night of March 31st, I announced that I would
not seek nor accept the nomination of my party for another
term as President.

I have devoted every resource of the Presidency to the
search for peace in Southeast Asia. Throughout the entire
summer and fall I have kept all of the presidential candidates fully briefed on developments in Paris as well as in
Vietnam. I have made it abundantly clear that no one candidate would have the advantage over others—either in information about those developments, or in advance notice
of the policy the Government intended to follow. The chief
diplomatic and military officers of this Government all
were instructed to follow the same course.

Since that night on March 31st, each of the candidates
has had differing ideas about the Government's policy. But
generally speaking, however, throughout the campaign we

have been able to present a united voice supporting our Government and supporting our men in Vietnam. I hope, and I believe, that this can continue until January 20th of next year when a new President takes office. Because in this critical hour, we just simply cannot afford more than one voice speaking for our Nation in the search for peace.

I do not know who will be inaugurated as the 37th President of the United States next January. But I do know that I shall do all that I can in the next few months to try to lighten his burdens as the contributions of the Presidents who preceded me have greatly lightened mine. I shall do everything in my power to move us toward the peace that the new President—as well as this President and, I believe, every other American—so deeply and urgently desires.

To Win Peace, America Must Keep Fighting

Richard Nixon

In the fall of 1969 America was a place of turmoil. Hundreds of thousands of people, all over the country, took part in antiwar protests and demonstrations. President Richard Nixon responded by stepping in front of the television cameras on November 3, 1969, and bringing his case directly to the people. In his address to the nation, which is excerpted below, Nixon appeals to "the great silent majority" to help him end the war. He outlines the situation in Vietnam, including the obstacles to peace. He says that early withdrawal will negatively affect the Paris peace talks, and he reveals a new war strategy that relies less on American infantry and more on troops from South Vietnam, a strategy he calls the "Vietnamization" of the war. In the days that followed this address, telegrams and letters of support flooded the White House; the "silent majority" had responded loudly and clearly. Nixon was the thirty-seventh president of the United States, serving from 1969 until his post-Watergate resignation in 1974.

As you read, consider the following questions:
1. What does Nixon mean by "the silent majority"?
2. Why does Nixon think the United States should not withdraw immediately from the conflict in Vietnam?
3. What reasons does Nixon give for not offering a clear time line for American withdrawal?

Richard Nixon, address to the American public, November 3, 1969.

Tonight I want to talk to you on a subject of deep concern to all Americans and to many people in all parts of the world—the war in Vietnam.

I believe that one of the reasons for the deep division about Vietnam is that many Americans have lost confidence in what their Government has told them about our policy. The American people cannot and should not be asked to support a policy which involves the overriding issues of war and peace unless they know the truth about that policy.

Tonight, therefore, I would like to answer some of the questions that I know are on the minds of many of you listening to me. How and why did America get involved in Vietnam in the first place? How has this administration changed the policy of the previous administration? What has really happened in the negotiations in Paris and on the battlefront in Vietnam? What choices do we have if we are to end the war? What are the prospects for peace? Now, let me begin by describing the situation I found when I was inaugurated on January 20 [1969]:

The war had been going on for four years. One thousand Americans had been killed in action. The training program for the South Vietnamese was behind schedule; 540,000 Americans were in Vietnam with no plans to reduce the number. No progress had been made at the negotiations in Paris and the United States had not put forth a comprehensive peace proposal. The war was causing deep division at home and criticism from many of our friends as well as our enemies abroad.

In view of these circumstances there were some who urged that I end the war at once by ordering the immediate withdrawal of all American forces. From a political standpoint this would have been a popular and easy course to follow. After all, we became involved in the war while my predecessor [Lyndon Johnson] was in office. I could blame the defeat which would be the result of my action on him and come out as the peacemaker. Some put it to me quite bluntly: This was the only way to avoid allowing Johnson's war to become Nixon's war.

But I had a greater obligation than to think only of the years of my administration and of the next election. I had to think of the effect of my decision on the next generation and on the future of peace and freedom in America and in the world.

Let us all understand that the question before us is not whether some Americans are for peace and some Americans are against peace. The question at issue is not whether Johnson's war becomes Nixon's war. The great question is: How can we win America's peace?

The Roots of American Involvement

Well, let us turn now to the fundamental issue. Why and how did the United States become involved in Vietnam in the first place? Fifteen years ago North Vietnam, with the logistical support of communist China and the Soviet Union, launched a campaign to impose a communist government on South Vietnam by instigating and supporting a revolution.

In response to the request of the Government of South Vietnam, President [Dwight] Eisenhower sent economic aid and military equipment to assist the people of South Vietnam in their efforts to prevent a communist takeover. Seven years ago [1962], President [John F.] Kennedy sent 16,000 military personnel to Vietnam as combat advisers. Four years ago [1965], President Johnson sent American combat forces to South Vietnam.

Now, many believe that President Johnson's decision to send American combat forces to South Vietnam was wrong. And many others—I among them—have been strongly critical of the way the war has been conducted.

But the question facing us today is: Now that we are in the war, what is the best way to end it?

The Perils of Withdrawing

In January [1969] I could only conclude that the precipitate withdrawal of American forces from Vietnam would be a disaster not only for South Vietnam but for the United

States and for the cause of peace.

For the South Vietnamese, our precipitate withdrawal would inevitably allow the Communists to repeat the massacres which followed their takeover in the North 15 years before; they then murdered more than 50,000 people and hundreds of thousands more died in slave labor camps.

We saw a prelude of what would happen in South Vietnam when the Communists entered the city of Hue last year. During their brief rule there, there was a bloody reign of terror in which 3,000 civilians were clubbed, shot to death, and buried in mass graves.

With the sudden collapse of our support, these atrocities of Hue would become the nightmare of the entire nation—and particularly for the million and a half Catholic refugees who fled to South Vietnam when the Communists took over in the North.

For the United States, this first defeat in our nation's history would result in a collapse of confidence in American leadership, not only in Asia but throughout the world.

Three American presidents have recognized the great stakes involved in Vietnam and understood what had to be done.

In 1963, President Kennedy, with his characteristic eloquence and clarity, said:

> . . . we want to see a stable government there, carrying on a struggle to maintain its national independence. We believe strongly in that. We are not going to withdraw from that effort. In my opinion, for us to withdraw from that effort would mean a collapse not only of South Vietnam, but Southeast Asia. So we are going to stay there.

President Eisenhower and President Johnson expressed the same conclusion during their terms of office.

For the future of peace, precipitate withdrawal would thus be a disaster of immense magnitude. A nation cannot remain great if it betrays its allies and lets down its friends.

Our defeat and humiliation in South Vietnam without question would promote recklessness in the councils of those great powers who have not yet abandoned their goals of world conquest. This would spark violence wherever our commitments help maintain the peace—in the Middle East, in Berlin, eventually even in the Western Hemisphere. Ultimately, this would cost more lives. It would not bring peace; it would bring more war.

Proposals for Peace

For these reasons, I rejected the recommendation that I should end the war by immediately withdrawing all of our forces. I chose instead to change American policy on both the negotiating front and battlefront. In order to end a war fought on many fronts, I initiated a pursuit for peace on many fronts. In a television speech on May 14 [1969], in a speech before the United Nations, and on a number of other occasions I set forth our peace proposals in great detail.

We have offered the complete withdrawal of all outside forces within one year.

We have proposed a cease-fire under international supervision.

We have offered free elections under international supervision with the Communists participating in the organization and conduct of the elections as an organized political force. And the Saigon Government has pledged to accept the result of the elections.

We have not put forth our proposals on a take-it-or-leave-it basis. We have indicated that we are willing to discuss the proposals that have been put forth by the other side. We have declared that anything is negotiable except the right of the people of South Vietnam to determine their own future. At the Paris peace conference, Ambassador [Henry Cabot] Lodge has demonstrated our flexibility and good faith in 40 public meetings.

Hanoi has refused even to discuss our proposals. They demand our unconditional acceptance of their terms, which are that we withdraw all American forces immediately and unconditionally and that we overthrow the Government of South Vietnam as we leave.

We have not limited our peace initiatives to public forums and public statements. I recognized, in January, that a long and bitter war like this usually cannot be settled in a public forum. That is why in addition to the public statements and negotiation I have explored every possible private avenue that might lead to a settlement. . . .

Peace Rejected

But the effect of all the public, private and secret negotiations which have been undertaken since the bombing halt a year ago and since this administration came into office on January 20 can be summed up in one sentence: No progress whatever has been made except agreement on the shape of the bargaining table.

Well now, who is at fault?

It has become clear that the obstacle in negotiating an end to the war is not the President of the United States. It is not the South Vietnamese Government.

The obstacle is the other side's absolute refusal to show the least willingness to join us in seeking a just peace. And it will not do so while it is convinced that all it has to do is to wait for our next concession, and our next concession after that one, until it gets everything it wants.

There can now be no longer any question that progress in negotiation depends only on Hanoi's deciding to negotiate, to negotiate seriously.

I realize that this report on our efforts on the diplomatic front is discouraging to the American people, but the American people are entitled to know the truth—the bad news as well as the good news—where the lives of our young men are involved.

Now let me turn, however, to a more encouraging report on another front.

At the time we launched our search for peace I recognized we might not succeed in bringing an end to the war through negotiation. I, therefore, put into effect another plan to bring peace—a plan which will bring the war to an end regardless of what happens on the negotiating front.

A New Foreign Policy

It is in line with a major shift in U.S. foreign policy which I described in my press conference at Guam on July 25. Let me briefly explain what has been described as the Nixon Doctrine—policy which not only will help end the war in Vietnam, but which is an essential element of our program to prevent future Vietnams.

We Americans are a do-it-yourself people. We are an impatient people. Instead of teaching someone else to do a job, we like to do it ourselves. And this trait has been carried over into our foreign policy. In Korea and again in Vietnam, the United States furnished most of the money, most of the arms, and most of the men to help the people of those countries defend their freedom against Communist aggression.

Before any American troops were committed to Vietnam, a leader of another Asian country expressed this opinion to me when I was traveling in Asia as a private citizen. He said: "When you are trying to assist another nation defend its freedom, U.S. policy should be to help them fight the war but not to fight the war for them."

Well, in accordance with this wise counsel, I laid down in Guam three principles as guidelines for future American policy toward Asia:

First, the United States will keep all of its treaty commitments.

Second, we shall provide a shield if a nuclear power threatens the freedom of a nation allied with us or of a nation whose survival we consider vital to our security.

Third, in cases involving other types of aggression, we shall furnish military and economic assistance when requested in accordance with our treaty commitments. But we shall look to the nation directly threatened to assume the primary responsibility of providing the manpower for its defense.

After I announced this policy, I found that the leaders of the Philippines, Thailand, Vietnam, South Korea, and other nations which might be threatened by Communist aggression welcomed this new direction in American foreign policy.

The defense of freedom is everybody's business—not just America's business. And it is particularly the responsibility of the people whose freedom is threatened. In the previous administration, we Americanized the war in Vietnam. In this administration, we are Vietnamizing the search for peace. . . .

Bringing Americans Home

We have adopted a plan which we have worked out in cooperation with the South Vietnamese for the complete withdrawal of all U.S. combat ground forces, and their replacement by South Vietnamese forces on an orderly scheduled timetable. This withdrawal will be made from strength and not from weakness. As South Vietnamese forces become stronger, the rate of American withdrawal can become greater.

I have not and do not intend to announce the timetable for our program. And there are obvious reasons for this decision which I am sure you will understand. As I have indicated on several occasions, the rate of withdrawal will depend on developments on three fronts.

One of these is the progress which can be or might be made in the Paris talks. An announcement of a fixed timetable for our withdrawal would completely remove any incentive for the enemy to negotiate an agreement. They would simply wait until our forces had withdrawn and then move in.

The other two factors on which we will base our withdrawal decisions are the level of enemy activity and the progress of the training programs of the South Vietnamese forces. And I am glad to be able to report tonight progress on both of these fronts has been greater than we anticipated when we started the program in June for withdrawal. As a result, our timetable for withdrawal is more optimistic now than when we made our first estimates in June. Now, this clearly demonstrates why it is not wise to be frozen in on a fixed timetable.

We must retain the flexibility to base each withdrawal decision on the situation as it is at that time rather than on estimates that are no longer valid.

Along with this optimistic estimate, I must—in all candor—leave one note of caution. If the level of enemy activity significantly increases we might have to adjust our timetable accordingly. . . .

Hanoi could make no greater mistake than to assume that an increase in violence will be to its advantage. If I conclude that increased enemy action jeopardizes our remaining forces in Vietnam, I shall not hesitate to take strong and effective measures to deal with that situation.

This is not a threat. This is a statement of policy, which as commander in chief of our armed forces, I am making in meeting my responsibility for the protection of American fighting men wherever they may be.

The Choice America Faces

My fellow Americans, I am sure you can recognize from what I have said that we really only have two choices open to us if we want to end this war.

I can order an immediate, precipitate withdrawal of all Americans from Vietnam without regard to the effects of that action. Or we can persist in our search for a just peace through a negotiated settlement if possible, or through continued implementation of our plan for Vietnamization if necessary, a plan in which we will withdraw all of our forces from Vietnam on a schedule in accordance with our program, as the South Vietnamese become strong enough to defend their own freedom.

I have chosen this second course. It is not the easy way. It is the right way.

It is a plan which will end the war and serve the cause of peace—not just in Vietnam but in the Pacific and in the world.

In speaking of the consequences of a precipitate withdrawal, I mentioned that our allies would lose confidence in America.

Far more dangerous, we would lose confidence in ourselves. Oh, the immediate reaction would be a sense of relief that our men were coming home. But as we saw the consequences of what we had done, inevitable remorse and divisive recrimination would scar our spirit as a people.

We have faced other crises in our history and have become stronger by rejecting the easy way out and taking the right way in meeting our challenges. Our greatness as a nation has been our capacity to do what had to be done when we knew our course was right.

I recognize that some of my fellow citizens disagree with the plan for peace I have chosen. Honest and patriotic Americans have reached different conclusions as to how peace should be achieved.

In San Francisco a few weeks ago, I saw demonstrators carrying signs reading: "Lose in Vietnam, bring the boys home."

Well, one of the strengths of our free society is that any American has a right to reach that conclusion and to advocate that point of view. But as president of the United States, I would be untrue to my oath of office if I allowed the policy of this nation to be dictated by the minority who hold that point of view and who try to impose it on the nation by mounting demonstrations in the street.

For almost 200 years, the policy of this nation has been made under our Constitution by those leaders in the Congress and the White House elected by all of the people. If a vocal minority, however fervent its cause, prevails over reason and the will of the majority, this nation has no future as a free society.

Vietnam Protesters

And now I would like to address a word, if I may, to the young people of this nation who are particularly concerned, and I understand why they are concerned, about this war.

I respect your idealism. I share your concern for peace. I want peace as much as you do. There are powerful personal reasons I want to end this war. This week I will have to sign 83 letters to mothers, fathers, wives and loved ones of men who have given their lives for America in Vietnam. It is very little satisfaction to me that this is only one-third as many letters as I signed the first week in office. There is nothing I want more than to see the day come when I do not have to write any of those letters.

I want to end the war to save the lives of those brave young men in Vietnam.

But I want to end it in a way which will increase the chance that their younger brothers and their sons will not have to fight in some future Vietnam someplace in the world.

And I want to end the war for another reason. I want to end it so that the energy and dedication of you, our young people, now too often directed into bitter hatred against those responsible for the war, can be turned to the great challenges of peace, a better life for all Americans, a better life for all people on this Earth. . . .

And so tonight—to you, the great silent majority of my fellow Americans—I ask for your support.

I pledged in my campaign for the presidency to end the war in a way that we could win the peace. I have initiated a plan of action which will enable me to keep that pledge.

The more support I can have from the American people, the sooner that pledge can be redeemed; for the more divided we are at home, the less likely the enemy is to negotiate at Paris.

Let us be united for peace. Let us also be united against defeat.

A Great Victory for a Great Nation

Van Tien Dung

When the last American troops pulled out of Vietnam on March 29, 1973, the war continued between North and South Vietnam and between South Vietnam and the Vietcong, or Communist revolutionaries, within the country. The final offensive of the war was launched in March 1975, when Communist forces under General Van Tien Dung pushed toward Saigon. The following excerpt from Van Tien Dung's book *Our Great Spring Victory* gives his account of the fall of Saigon, which occurred on April 30, 1975.

As you read, consider the following questions:
1. To what does Van Tien Dung attribute the Communist victory?
2. According to Van Tien Dung, what role did the people of South Vietnam play in the fall of Saigon?
3. What challenges does Van Tien Dung think the future will bring?

When it was almost light, the American news services reported that [U.S. ambassador Graham] Martin had cleared out of Saigon in a helicopter. This viceregal mandarin, the final American plenipotentiary in South Vietnam, beat a most hasty and pitiful retreat. As it happened, up until the day he left Saigon, Martin still felt certain that the quisling administration could be preserved, and that a ceasefire could be arranged, so he was halfhearted about the evacuation, waiting and watching. He went all the way out to Tan

Van Tien Dung, *Our Great Spring Victory: An Account of the Liberation of South Vietnam*, translated by John Spragens. New York: Monthly Review Press, 1977. Copyright © 1977 by Cora Weiss. Reproduced by permission of the publisher.

Son Nhat airfield to observe the situation. Our barrage of bombs and our fierce shelling had nearly paralyzed this vital airfield, and the fixed-wing aircraft they had intended to use for their evacuation could no longer operate. The encirclement of Saigon was growing tighter by the day. The Duong Van Minh card [a reference to putting Minh in power] which they had played far too late proved useless. When Martin reported this to Washington, President [Gerald] Ford issued orders to begin a helicopter evacuation. Coming in waves for eighteen hours straight, they carried more than 1,000 Americans and over 5,000 of their Vietnamese retainers, along with their families, out of the South. Ford also ordered Martin to evacuate immediately "without a minute's delay."

The U.S. Pulls Out

The American evacuation was carried out from the tops of thirteen tall buildings chosen as landing pads for their helicopters, The number of these landing pads shrank gradually as tongues of fire from our advancing troops came closer. At the American embassy, the boarding point for the evacuation copters was a scene of monumental confusion, with the Americans' flunkies fighting their way in, smashing doors, climbing walls, climbing each other's backs, tussling, brawling, and trampling each other as they sought to flee. It reached the point where Martin, who wanted to return to his own house for his suitcase before he fled, had to take a back street, using the rear gate of the embassy. When "Code 2," Martin's code name, and "Lady 09," the name of the helicopter carrying him, left the embassy for the East Sea, it signaled the shameful defeat of U.S. imperialism after thirty years of intervention and military adventures in Vietnam. At the height of their invasion of Vietnam, the U.S. had used 60 percent of their total infantry, 58 percent of their marines, 32 percent of their tactical air force, 50 percent of their strategic air force, fifteen of their eighteen aircraft carriers, 800,000 American troops (counting those stationed in satellite countries who were taking part in the

Vietnam war), and more than 1 million Saigon troops. They mobilized as many as 6 million American soldiers in rotation, dropped over 10 million tons of bombs, and spent over $300 billion, but in the end the U.S. ambassador had to crawl up to the helicopter pad looking for a way to flee. Today, looking back on the gigantic force the enemy had mobilized, recalling the malicious designs they admitted, and thinking about the extreme difficulties and complexities which our revolutionary sampan had had to pass through, we were all the more aware how immeasurably great this campaign to liberate Saigon and liberate the South was. . . .

The Source of Inspiration

The most extraordinary thing about this historic campaign was what had sprouted in the souls of our cadres and fighters. Why were our soldiers so heroic and determined during this campaign? What had given all of them this clear understanding of the great resolution of the party and of the nation, this clear understanding of our immeasurably precious opportunity, and this clear understanding of our unprecedented manner of fighting? What had made them so extraordinarily courageous and intense, so outstanding in their political acumen in this final phase of the war?

The will and competence of our soldiers were not achieved in a day, but were the result of a continuous process of carrying out the party's ideological and organizational work in the armed forces. And throughout our thirty years of struggle, there had been no campaign in which Uncle Ho [Ho Chi Minh] had not gone into the operation with our soldiers. Going out to battle this time, our whole army had been given singular, unprecedented strength because this strategically decisive battle bore his name: Ho Chi Minh, for every one of our cadres and fighters, was faith, strength, and life. Among the myriad troops in all the advancing wings, every one of our fighters carried toward Ho Chi Minh City the hopes of the nation and a love for our land. Today each fighter could see with his own eyes the resiliency which the Fatherland had built up during these many years, and given his own resiliency there was nothing, no enemy scheme that could stop him.

Our troops advanced rapidly to the five primary objectives, and then spread out from there. Wherever they went, a forest of revolutionary flags appeared, and people poured out to cheer them, turning the streets of Saigon into a giant festival. From the Binh Phoc bridge to Quan Tre, people carrying flags, beating drums and hollow wooden fish, and calling through megaphones, chased down the enemy, disarmed enemy soldiers, neutralized traitors and spies, and guided our soldiers. In Hoc Mon on Route 1, the people all came out into the road to greet the soldiers, guide them, and point out the hiding places of enemy thugs. Everywhere people used megaphones to call on Saigon soldiers to take off their uniforms and lay down their guns. The people of the city, especially the workers, protected factories and warehouses and turned them over to our soldiers. In all the districts bordering the city—Binh Hoa, Thanh My Tay, Phu Nhuan, Go Vap, and Thu Duc—members of the revolutionary infrastructure and other people distributed leaflets, raised flags, called on enemy soldiers to drop their guns, and supplied and guided our soldiers. Before this great army entered the city, the great cause of our nation and the policies of our revolution had entered the hearts of the people.

The Support of the People

We were very pleased to hear that the people of the city rose up when the military attacks, going one step ahead, had given them the leverage. The masses had entered this decisive battle at just the right time, not too early, but not too late. The patriotic actions of the people created a revolutionary atmosphere of vast strength on all the city's streets. This was the most precious aspect of the mass movement in Saigon-Gia Dinh, the result of many years of propaganda, education, organizing, and training by the municipal party branch. When the opportune moment arrived, those political troops had risen up with a vanguard spirit, and advanced in giant strides along with our powerful main-force divisions, resolutely, intelligently, and courageously. The people of the city not only carried flags and food and drink for the troops, but helped disperse large numbers of enemy soldiers, forced many to surrender, chased and captured many of those who were hiding out, and preserved order and security in the streets. And we will never forget the widespread and moving images of thousands, of tens of thousands of people enthusiastically giving directions to our soldiers and guiding them as they entered the city, and helping all the wings of troops strike quickly and unexpectedly at enemy positions. Those nameless heroes of Saigon-Gia Dinh brought into the general offensive the fresh and beautiful features of people's war.

As we looked at the combat operations map, the five wings of our troops seemed like five lotuses blossoming out from our five major objectives. The First Army Corps had captured Saigon's General Staff headquarters and the command compounds of all the enemy armed services. When the Third Army Corps captured Tan Son Nhat they met one wing of troops already encamped there—our military delegation at Camp Davis; it was an amazing and moving meeting. The Fourth Army Corps captured Saigon's Ministry of Defense, the Bach Dang port, and the radio station. The 232nd force took the Special Capital Zone headquarters and the Directorate-General of Police. The Second Army Corps seized "Independence Palace," the place where the quisling leaders, those hirelings of the United States, had sold our independence, traded in human blood, and carried on their smuggling. Our soldiers immediately rushed upstairs to the place where the quisling cabinet was meeting, and arrested the whole central leadership of the Saigon administration, including their president, right on the spot. Our soldiers' vigorous actions and firm declarations revealed the spirit of a victorious army. By 11:30 A.M. on April 30 the revolutionary flag flew from "Independence Palace"; this became the meeting point for all the wings of liberating troops.

At the front headquarters, we turned on our radios to listen. The voice of the quisling president called on his troops to put down their weapons and surrender unconditionally to our troops. Saigon was completely liberated! Total victory! We were completely victorious! All of us at headquarters jumped up and shouted, embraced and carried each other around on our shoulders. The sound of applause, laughter, and happy, noisy, chattering speech was as festive as if spring had just burst upon us. It was an indescribably joyous scene. Le Duc Tho and Pham Hung [two members of the North Vietnamese politburo] embraced me and all the cadres and fighters present. We were all so happy we were choked with emotion. I lit a cigarette and smoked. Dinh Duc Thien [a member of the North Vietnamese politburo], his eyes somewhat red, said, "Now if these eyes close, my heart will be at rest." This historic and sacred, intoxicating and completely satisfying moment was one that comes once in a generation, once in many generations. Our generation had known many victorious mornings, but there had been no morning so fresh and beautiful, so radiant, so clear and cool, so sweet-scented as this morning of total victory, a morning which made babes older than their years and made old men young again. . . .

Looking to the Future

Le Duc Tho, Pham Hung, and I leaned on our chairs looking at the map of Ho Chi Minh City [as Saigon was renamed] spread out on the table. We thought of the welter of jobs ahead. Were the electricity and water in Saigon still working? Saigon's army of nearly 1 million had disbanded on the spot. How should we deal with them? What could we do to help the hungry and find ways for the millions of unemployed to make a living? Should we ask the center to send in supplies right away to keep the factories in Saigon alive? How could we quickly build up a revolutionary administration at the grassroots level? What policy should we take toward the bourgeoisie? And how could we carry the

South on to socialism along with the whole country? The conclusion of this struggle was the opening of another, no less complex and filled with hardship. The difficulties would be many, but the advantages were not few. Saigon and the South, which had gone out first and returned last, deserved a life of peace, plenty, and happiness. . . .

We took a car to Saigon, past areas and positions so vital for the liberation of the city, like Trang Bang and Cu Chi, and past areas which had been revolutionary bases for many years, since the founding of the party, like Hoc Mon and Ba Diem. Along the highway, in the villages, and in the city streets there was no sea of blood, only a sea of people in high spirits, waving their hands and waving flags to welcome peace and the revolution. That sea of people, mingling endlessly with the long lines of our soldiers' trucks, tanks, and cars, in itself proclaimed our total victory. The sides of the road were still clogged with uniforms, rank insignia, guns and ammunition, boots, helmets, vehicles, and artillery the puppet army had abandoned in defeat. Spread out around us were not only the relics of a military force that had been smashed, but the relics of a reactionary political doctrine that had unraveled, the doctrine of a crew of imperialists so arrogant about their wealth and so worshipful of possessions that it blinded them. It was ironic that at every enemy base and barracks a sign had been erected, painted in large letters with the words, "Honor-Responsibility-Fatherland." What the enemy did not have, they had to shout about loudest. The main road into Saigon was very good, built by the enemy in the past to serve their operations. All of the enemy bases and storage depots were vast. The banks, the American billets, the hotels, many stories tall, were imposing advertisements for neocolonialism, implying that it would stand firm here, that it would stand for time without end. In 1968 [American general William] Westmoreland boasted, "We will always be in Vietnam. Our bombs and bullets will prove it." But in fact the proof was exactly the opposite. We went into the headquarters of Saigon's General Staff. Here, as at the enemy Directorate-General of Police, the files of the enemy commanders' top secret documents remained. Their modern computer with its famous memory containing bio-data on each officer and soldier in their million-plus army was still running. American computers had not won in this war. The intelligence and will of our nation had won completely.

CHRONOLOGY

1945

In March the Japanese depose the French colonial rulers of Vietnam and take control of the country. On September 2, the same day the Japanese sign a surrender agreement concluding World War II, Ho Chi Minh proclaims Vietnamese independence. In October, with the support of the British, the French regain control of much of Vietnam.

1946

In December the Vietminh launch their first major attack against the French, with whom they have fought skirmishes throughout the year. Thus begins the First Indochina War, which lasts eight years.

1949

In October Mao Zedong's Communist forces defeat the Nationalist army of Chiang Kai-shek, leading to fear within the United States of Communist domination of all of Southeast Asia.

1950

In January China and the Soviet Union recognize the Democratic Republic of Vietnam, led by Ho Chi Minh, and China ships military equipment to the Vietminh. In February the United States and Britain recognize the Bao Dai government in South Vietnam. In July American president Harry Truman offers the French in Vietnam $15 million in military aid, which is the start of U.S. military involvement.

1953

American president Dwight Eisenhower invokes the Domino Theory to justify continued U.S. military support for the

French in Vietnam, who are fighting the Vietminh. According to the theory, if even a single country in Southeast Asia fell to communism, the entire region would quickly be lost to dictatorship.

1954

In May Dien Bien Phu falls, ending French rule in Vietnam. Forty thousand Vietminh troops lay siege to the French military garrison and shell its airstrip, cutting off all supply routes and forcing the French surrender. In July the Geneva Convention divides Vietnam at the seventeenth parallel into North Vietnam, led by Ho Chi Minh, and South Vietnam, led by Emperor Bao Dai. The accords call for a general election to reunite the country within two years.

1955

In October South Vietnamese prime minister Ngo Dinh Diem replaces Emperor Bao Dai in a rigged election.

1956

In July the deadline passes for the elections meant to unify Vietnam. President Diem of South Vietnam refuses to participate, fearing a Communist victory.

1957

In January the Soviet Union proposes the division between North and South Vietnam be accepted as permanent, with both countries accepted into the United Nations. The United States refuses. In October the Vietminh begin a guerrilla campaign in South Vietnam, targeting South Vietnamese officials, of whom more than four hundred are killed by the end of the year.

1959

President Ngo Dinh Diem cracks down on Communists and other dissidents with harsh new laws.

1960

In April North Vietnam imposes universal conscription. In South Vietnam, President Diem shuts down several opposition newspapers and arrests journalists and intellectuals. In November Diem orders a further crackdown on "enemies of the state"; more than fifty thousand are arrested. In December the National Liberation Front, a revolutionary group, is formed in South Vietnam. President Diem calls them the "Vietcong," a dismissive term that means "Vietnamese Communist."

1961

In January Soviet premier Nikita Khrushchev promises that the USSR will support all "wars of national liberation," which encourages the Vietcong in their fight against Diem. In May American president John F. Kennedy sends four hundred American troops to South Vietnam to serve as "special advisers" training South Vietnamese soldiers.

1962

In August U.S. president Kennedy signs the Foreign Assistance Act, which pledges "military assistance to countries which are on the rim of the Communist world and under direct attack."

1963

Public resistance to the government of Ngo Dinh Diem mounts. Throughout the summer, Buddhists protest Diem's religious intolerance with public rallies and, on several occasions, by self-immolation. Diem responds by imposing martial law. In November, with the quiet approval of the United States, a coup by the South Vietnamese army deposes Diem, who is subsequently killed along with his brother Ngo Dinh Nhu.

1964

In March U.S. defense secretary Robert McNamara visits South Vietnam and pledges that the United States will "stay for as long as it takes" to defeat the Communist insurgents. On July 31 South Vietnamese troops in unmarked speed boats raid two North Vietnamese military bases in the Gulf of Tonkin. On August 2 three North Vietnamese patrol boats fire torpedoes and machine-gun rounds at the USS *Maddox* in the Gulf of Tonkin. On August 3 the USS *Maddox* and the USS *C. Turner Joy* begin an aggressive series of movements in the Gulf of Tonkin. That night, with the accuracy of their electronic instruments diminished by thunderstorms, crew members take themselves to be under attack and return fire. On August 4, although there are serious doubts about whether the second attack occurred, the United States bombs oil facilities and naval targets in North Vietnam. On August 7 the U.S. Congress passes the Gulf of Tonkin Resolution, giving the president the power to "take all necessary steps, including the use of armed force" to protect American troops stationed in the area.

1965

In March the United States commences Operation Rolling Thunder, an air campaign against North Vietnam. The first combat troops, a contingent of 3,500 U.S. Marines, arrives to join 23,000 American military advisers. American president Lyndon Johnson authorizes the use of napalm. In May the United States announces a pause in bombing in the hope that North Vietnam will negotiate; the pause lasts six days. In July Johnson announces he is sending forty-four combat battalions to Vietnam, bringing the total number of American troops to 125,000. In August Johnson signs a bill making it illegal to burn draft cards. In December he announces a second bombing pause, which lasts thirty-seven days. By year's end there are 184,300 American troops in Vietnam.

1966

In February the Senate Foreign Relations Committee holds televised hearings on American involvement in Vietnam. In March an attempt to repeal the Gulf of Tonkin Resolution fails in the Senate by a vote of ninety-two to five. Antiwar protests are held in Washington, New York, Chicago, Boston, San Francisco, and Philadelphia. In October the Soviet Union announces economic and military support for North Vietnam. By the end of the year, there are 389,000 American soldiers in Vietnam. Just over 5,000 U.S. troops are killed, and 30,000 are wounded.

1967

In February Operation Junction City, the largest American military offensive of the war, begins with twenty-two American battalions and four South Vietnamese battalions. 2,728 Vietcong are killed, as are 282 Americans. In April there are huge demonstrations against the war in New York and San Francisco, with Martin Luther King Jr. saying that the war is detracting from President Johnson's planned social programs. In July General William Westmoreland, the American commander in Vietnam, asks for 200,000 more soldiers, which would bring the total commitment to 675,000. Johnson sends only 45,000 more. In November U.S. defense secretary Robert McNamara resigns, privately citing his concerns with President Johnson's war strategy. In December the Vietcong murder 252 civilians in the village of Dak Son, according to the U.S. military. At the end of the year, total American combat losses are approximately 16,000.

1968

In January 20,000 North Vietnamese troops lay siege to the American air base at Khe Sanh in the northernmost part of South Vietnam, home to 5,000 American soldiers. President Johnson, who is terrified of a repeat of the fall of Dien

Bien Phu, orders a massive bombardment of the North Vietnamese troops. On the final day of the month, Vietcong guerrillas launch the Tet Offensive, a coordinated attack on cities and towns throughout South Vietnam. Although the Vietcong suffer heavy losses, the offensive is considered a major setback to the United States. In the city of Hue, victorious Vietcong execute more than 3,000 South Vietnamese troops and government officials. In February the chairman of the U.S. Joint Chiefs of Staff asks President Johnson for 206,000 more troops, a request Secretary of State Dean Rusk denies was ever made after the *New York Times* breaks the story a week later. In March American soldiers massacre three hundred civilians in the village of My Lai. President Johnson announces he will not seek reelection and urges North Vietnam to negotiate, ordering a partial halt to bombing. In April the seventy-seven-day siege of Khe Sanh ends when North Vietnamese troops withdraw. In May peace talks begin in Paris but they soon flounder. In August 10,000 antiwar protesters at the Democratic National Convention are met by 26,000 police and National Guardsmen. Eight hundred protesters are injured. By the end of the year, there are 495,000 American soldiers in Vietnam and an accumulated American death toll of approximately 30,000.

1969

In January peace talks open again in Paris. In March U.S. president Richard Nixon authorizes the secret bombing of Communist supply sanctuaries in Cambodia. In April U.S. troop levels reach their highest point—543,000. In May forty-six American soldiers die during the battle for "Hamburger Hill." After they successfully take the hill, they are ordered to abandon it, at which point the North Vietnamese retake the hill without opposition. To many in the United States, the episode is a sign of the absurdity of the conflict. In June President Nixon announces the "Vietnamization" of the war, which calls for reducing the number of American soldiers involved. In September President Nixon orders the withdrawal of 35,000 troops. In November, 250,000 demonstrators gather in Washington to protest the war. In December 50,000 more U.S. troops leave Vietnam. By the end of the year, total U.S. deaths since the start of the war are 40,024.

1970

In April President Nixon announces the gradual withdrawal of another 150,000 U.S. troops. Just over a week later, when Nixon reveals that U.S. forces had entered Cambodia, protests erupt across the country. At Kent State University in Ohio, National Guardsmen kill four students and wound nine, which prompts protests that shut down four hundred colleges and universities around the country. In June the U.S. Senate repeals the 1964 Gulf of Tonkin Resolution. In December Congress bars the use of ground forces in Laos or Cambodia. By year's end, American troop levels have dropped to 280,000.

1971

In May twelve thousand protesters are arrested in Washington. In June the *New York Times* starts publishing *The Pentagon Papers*, an archive of classified paperwork documenting the decision making of previous administrations in regard to Vietnam. President Nixon asks a U.S. district court to halt publication in the *Times* and in the *Washington Post*, which starts to publish the documents as well. The U.S. Supreme Court rules against Nixon. By the end of the year, U.S. troop levels are down to 150,000.

1972

In February President Nixon visits Communist China, a major diplomatic accomplishment. In April, in response to the North Vietnamese Eastertide Offensive, Nixon orders massive bombing on North Vietnam; serious protests occur in the United States. In May Nixon authorizes Operation Linebacker, which calls for more bombing of North Vietnam and for the mining of North Vietnam's harbors. In May Nixon visits the Soviet Union to improve diplomatic relations. In August the last U.S. combat troops leave Vietnam. In December peace talks break down because North Vietnam rejects changes demanded by South Vietnam to an agreement forged between North Vietnam and the United States. Nixon launches what comes to be known as "the Christmas bombings," a massive bombardment of military targets in Hanoi.

1973

In January the United States, North Vietnam, South Vietnam, and the Vietcong sign the Paris Peace Accords, which ends American involvement and leaves Vietnam divided. On January 27 Lt. Col. William Nolde is killed; he is the last American soldier to die in combat in Vietnam. In June the U.S. Congress forbids any further American military action in Southeast Asia.

1974

In September U.S. president Gerald Ford announces a clemency program for deserted soldiers and those who evaded the draft.

1975

In March North Vietnamese troops push into South Vietnam, capturing cities on the march to Saigon with relative ease. On April 29 President Ford orders the helicopter evacuation of thousands of Americans from Saigon. On April 30, the last Americans withdraw from Saigon. Within hours, the Vietcong have taken control as the South Vietnamese president unconditionally surrenders. The war is over.

FOR FURTHER RESEARCH

Books

Trent Angers, *The Forgotten Hero of My Lai: The Hugh Thompson Story.* Lafayette, LA: Acadian House, 1999. A recounting of the actions of Hugh Thompson, an American helicopter pilot who intervened during the My Lai massacre to rescue Vietnamese civilians.

Michael Bilton and Kevin Sim, *Four Hours in My Lai.* New York: Viking, 1992. An account of the massacre of Vietnamese civilians at My Lai and of the subsequent cover-up.

William L. Calley, as told to John Sack, *Lieutenant Calley: His Own Story.* New York: Tempo, 1974. Calley was the platoon leader in My Lai who did most of the killings and the only person convicted by court-martial.

Allan Cameron, ed., *Vietnam Crisis: A Documentary History.* 2 vols. Ithaca, NY: Cornell University Press, 1971. A collection of primary documents.

Michael Charlton and Anthony Moncrieff, *Many Reasons Why: The American Involvement in Vietnam.* New York: Hill and Wang, 1978. Contains a series of interviews with high-ranking Americans.

Allan B. Cole, ed., *Conflict in Indo-China and International Repercussions: A Documentary History, 1945–1955.* Ithaca, NY: Cornell University Press, 1956. A collection of primary documents concerning the final years of French rule in Vietnam.

David Dellinger, *From Yale to Jail: The Life Story of a Moral Dissenter.* New York: Pantheon, 1993. Dellinger was a major figure in the antiwar movement.

Jeremiah Denton with Ed Brandt, *When Hell Was in Session*. Clover, SC: Commission, 1976. An account focusing on American prisoners of war.

William Dudley, ed., *The Vietnam War: Opposing Viewpoints*. San Diego: Greenhaven, 1998. A collection of articles written from diverse perspectives.

Horst Faas and Tim Page, eds., *Requiem: By the Photographers Who Died in Vietnam and Indochina*. New York: Random House, 1997. A collection of photographs taken by American and foreign photographers who were killed covering the Vietnam War.

Felix Greene, *Vietnam! Vietnam!* Palo Alto, CA: Fulton, 1966. A highly critical view of the war.

Daniel C. Hallin, *"The Uncensored War": The Media and Vietnam*. New York: Oxford University Press, 1986. A major analysis of media coverage of the war and of its effect on public opinion.

David Harris, *Our War: What We Did in Vietnam and What It Did to Us*. New York: Times Books, 1996. Harris, who was elected president of Stanford University's student council in 1966, became a leader of the antiwar movement and served twenty months in prison for resisting the draft.

Arnold Isaacs, *Without Honor: Defeat in Vietnam and Cambodia*. Baltimore: Johns Hopkins University Press, 1983. A thorough account of the final days of the war.

Stanley Karnow, *Vietnam: A History*. New York: Viking, 1983. A major and well-regarded work by a journalist that focuses on American involvement in Vietnam.

George Katsiaficas, ed., *Vietnam Documents: American and Vietnamese Views of the War*. Armonk, NY: M.E. Sharpe, 1992. A collection of primary documents covering American and Vietnamese (both North and South) perspectives.

Eugene McCarthy, *The Year of the People.* Garden City, NY: Doubleday, 1969. Dismayed with Johnson's Vietnam policy, McCarthy, a Democratic senator, ran against President Lyndon Johnson in the Democratic primaries preceding the 1968 presidential election.

The Pentagon Papers: The Defense Department History of United States Decisionmaking on Vietnam. 5 vols. Boston: Beacon, 1971. The Pentagon Papers was a top secret government study of the decision-making that led to the Vietnam War. When the study was leaked to the *New York Times* in 1971, the federal government fought to keep the newspaper from publishing the information, but the Supreme Court ultimately decided in favor of the newspaper and significant portions of the seven-thousand–plus page report were published.

John Clark Pratt, *Vietnam Voices: Perspectives on the War Years, 1941–1982.* New York: Penguin, 1984. A collection of primary documents.

Bertrand Russell, *War Crimes in Vietnam.* New York: Monthly Review, 1967. An elegantly written account by a leading twentieth-century philosopher and political activist.

Ronald Spector, *After Tet: The Bloodiest Year in Vietnam.* New York: Free, 1993. A focused look at 1968, which began with the Tet Offensive.

William Westmoreland, *A Soldier Reports.* New York: Doubleday, 1976. Westmoreland was commander of American forces in Vietnam from 1964 to 1968.

James Willwerth, *Eye in the Last Storm: A Reporter's Journal of One Year in Southeast Asia.* New York: Grossman, 1972. An account of what it was like to be a reporter in Vietnam (the author reported from Vietnam for *Time* magazine).

Howard Zinn, *Vietnam: The Logic of Withdrawal.* Boston: Beacon, 1967. Zinn, a professor at Boston University, was one of the most important academics to oppose the war.

Periodicals

Eddie Adams, "The Pictures That Burn in My Memory," *Parade*, May 15, 1983.

Atlantic Monthly, Vietnam report, August 1969.

Tom Buckley, "Portrait of an Aging Despot," *Harper's Magazine*, April 1972.

Ward S. Just, "Notes on Losing a War," *Atlantic Monthly*, January 1969.

Newsweek, "Do We Have a Chance to Win?" September 21, 1964.

———, "Hanoi Attacks," February 28, 1968.

———, "We Seek No Wider War," August 17, 1964.

Merlo J. Pusey, "The President and the Power to Make War," *Atlantic Monthly*, July 1969.

U.S. News & World Report, "The 'Phantom Battle' That Led to War," July 23, 1984.

David Wise, "Remember the *Maddox!*" *Esquire*, April 1968.

Websites

The American Experience: Vietnam Online, www.pbs.org. The site, published by the Public Broadcasting Service (PBS), includes transcripts of PBS's thirteen-part series, *Vietnam: A Television History*, a detailed time line, a who's who of key players in the conflict, maps, and other documents.

The Communist Party of Vietnam, www.cpv.org.vn. This page celebrates Ho Chi Minh, the Communist revolutionary and North Vietnamese leader.

Foreign Relations of the United States, www.state.gov. A publication of the U.S. State Department, this site has a huge number of primary documents relating to the diplomatic and political aspects of the Vietnam War.

Teach Vietnam: Echoes from the Wall, www.teachvietnam. org. This site, run by the Vietnam Veterans Memorial Fund, is designed for teachers and students. In addition to information, the site offers suggestions for teaching plans and student projects.

Vietnam Veterans Against the War, www.vvaw.org. The home page of the influential antiwar group, which remains active today.

Vietnam Veterans' Home Page, http://grunt.space.swri.edu. This site emphasizes the American veteran's perspective and includes personal narratives and remembrances as well as a large collection of articles and images.

The Vietnam War, www.vietnampix.com. A collection of photographs from the Vietnam War, most by photographer Tim Page.

The Vietnam War Internet Page, www.vwip.org. An extensive collection of information and documents, including memoirs and retrospectives, primary and secondary articles, and images. The site also has a thorough collection of links.

The Virtual Wall: A Digital Legacy Project for Remembrance, www.thevirtualwall.org. The site offers a virtual version of the Vietnam memorial wall in Washington, D.C., and includes veteran profiles, remembrances, reunion postings, name rubbings, and custom-generated reports.

The Wars for Vietnam: 1945–1975, http://vietnam.vassar. edu. A publication of Vassar College, this site includes a concise overview of the conflict and a collection of important primary documents.

INDEX

GI Civil Liberties Defense
  Committee, 161
Greenfield, James, 80
Gruver, Butch, 122, 123
Gulf of Tonkin
  American version on
    attack at, 60–61
  justification for U.S.
    response to, 62–63
  limited U.S. response to,
    62
  as part of North
    Vietnamese pattern, 63
  Soviet response to, 66–68
  U.S. as responsible for
    tension in, 68–69
Gulf of Tonkin Resolution
  (1964), 25, 57–58

Harriman, Averell, 188
Heinl, Robert D. Jr., 156
heroin use, 160
Ho Chi Minh, 31
  declaration of Vietnam's
    independence by, 31–34
  France and, 29
  as inspiration to
    Vietnamese soldiers, 208
  Tet Offensive and, 116
  would not adversely affect
    U.S. interests, 181
  see also North Vietnam
Honeycutt, Weldon, 159

"iron curtain," 13–14

Johnson, Lyndon, 23, 90,
  187

analysis of Johns Hopkins
  address by, 174–75
Cold War politics of, 24
on Domino Theory, 57
not seeking reelection,
  171–72
nuclear weapons and, 24
on threat of China, 91–92
use of American forces
  under, 23
on U.S. involvement in
  Vietnam, 90–91, 92–93
war powers of, 57–58

Kennedy, John F., 53
Kennedy administration
  Cuban missile crisis and,
    22
  Diem and, 57
  on the Domino Theory,
    54–55
  on U.S. support for South
    Vietnam, 22–23
  on withdrawal of U.S.
    troops, 198
Kent State University
  shooting (1970), 135
Kerry, John, 142
Khe Sanh military base,
  101
  change in U.S. tactics for,
    119–20
  closure of, 120
  Tet Offensive and, 114,
    115–16
  U.S. goals at, 119
Khrushchev, Nikita, 21, 22,
  66